SECOND

THE STARS

ASTRONOMY IN THE BIBLE

SPEAK

STEWART CUSTER

 BJU PRESS

Greenville, South Carolina

Library of Congress Cataloging-in-Publication Data

Custer, Stewart, 1931-
 The stars speak : astronomy in the Bible / Stewart Custer. —
2nd ed.
  p. cm.
 Includes bibliographical references (p.   ) and indexes.
 ISBN 1-57924-818-7
 1. Astronomy in the Bible.   I. Title.
BS655.C87 2002
220.8'52—dc21

2002010005

Cover image and interior color images courtesy of NASA.

Note: The fact that materials produced by other publishers may be referred to in this volume does not constitute an endorsement by Bob Jones University Press of the content or theological position of materials produced by such publishers. The position of Bob Jones University Press, and of the University itself, is well known. Any references and ancillary materials are listed as an aid to the reader and in an attempt to maintain the accepted academic standards of the publishing industry.

All Scripture is quoted from the Authorized King James Version unless otherwise noted.

NASV: Scripture taken from the NEW AMERICAN STANDARD VERSION ® Copyright © 1981 by Holman Bible Publishers. Scripture Text, References, and Concordance © 1960, 1962, 1963, 1968, 1971, 1972, 1973, 1975, 1977 by the Lockman Foundation. Used by permission.

Designed by TJ Getz
Composition by Bonnijean Marley
Interior illustrations by Bessie A. Custer

© 2002 by Bob Jones University Press
Greenville, SC 29614

Printed in the United States of America
All rights reserved

ISBN 1-57924-818-7

15 14 13 12 11 10 9 8 7 6 5 4 3 2

To my
mother and father,
who early taught me
to love both
the Bible and the stars

Symbols of Brightness: Magnitude

-0   1 2 3 4 5

Nebulae ○

CONTENTS

PREFACE

The last major study of biblical references to the astronomical objects was E. Walter Maunder's *The Astronomy of the Bible* in 1909. Of course, it has been out of print for many years, not to say outdated. Most of the topics covered in the following pages I have presented to audiences in programs at the Howell Memorial Planetarium at Bob Jones University. The University has manifested great wisdom in giving a strong emphasis upon both the teaching of Scripture and a broad spectrum of liberal arts. Such interdisciplinary investigation has been highly beneficial to generations of students. Many members of planetarium audiences have asked questions about truths from both science and the Bible. Many of them have also suggested that the answers be put in print so that a wider audience could share in the fascination of such discoveries. The present book is a direct result of the interest of those kind audiences. Ever since 1960 I have had the joy of writing and presenting these topics to audiences and I hope that my interest in the stars and in the Scriptures strikes a responsive chord in many readers.

The following chapters have retained their original format as self-sufficient units, though with an intended cumulative effect: the reader's sense of the immensity of the universe should increase from chapter to chapter. Basic astronomical background will be introduced from time to time as needed. Searching the night skies for hidden wonders brings the joy of many discoveries, just as searching the Scriptures brings joy. May the following pages bring the wonder of discovery to the reader, and may his delight in hidden truths, both of science and of Scripture, increase page by page. May he come to know "the wonder and glory of the universe" and the God who created all things.

I am indebted to Dr. Ronald Horton for numerous suggestions for the improvement of style and logic. I also am indebted to my mother for the meticulous drawings of astronomical objects that illustrate the following pages, and to my father for one of my earliest memories, of sitting on his shoulder and looking up as he pointed out the Big Dipper and the North Star for the very first time. The wonder of that moment has never left me.

S. C.

WHEN I CONSIDER THY HEAVENS, THE WORK OF THY
FINGERS, THE MOON AND THE STARS, WHICH THOU
HAST ORDAINED; WHAT IS MAN, THAT THOU ART
MINDFUL OF HIM?

PSALM 8:3-4

Stars and dust clouds in Monoceros

The Wonder
of It All

How can a frog sing underwater? Why do a pigeon's bones weigh less than its feathers? How many eggs can a codfish lay at one time? What is the longest river in the world? Men have always delighted in such questions and have spent great effort in learning the answers. The wonders of astronomy are among the most curious and fascinating facts of nature. Astronomers have learned that there are objects in the universe that are hotter or colder than anything we know on earth. The mind of man staggers at the distances and sizes of the celestial objects. He wonders whether there is life elsewhere in the universe. He wonders why there is an apparent eleven-year sunspot cycle. He wonders what the Great Red Spot is on the planet Jupiter. He wonders why all the temples of ancient Egypt were aligned with the sun, moon, or a specific star or planet.

The pages that follow survey the major topics of astronomy and will transport the reader from the observations of the ancient Babylonians to the travels of the astronauts. The star charts locate the stars and constellations of every season of the year. Discussions of the stars identify them also by size, color, and temperature. A unique feature of the book is the correlation between science and the Scriptures.

The importance of the heavenly bodies is evident in their frequent appearance in the Scriptures. Unfortunately, of the more than three hundred biblical references to astronomical objects, most serious students of the Bible would have trouble naming a dozen. What is the first verse in the Bible that names the stars? What is meant by the "stars in their courses fought against Sisera" (Judg. 5:20)? Who labored to rebuild the ancient walls of Jerusalem "from the rising of the morning till the stars appeared"(Neh. 4:21)? Who was caught by a fierce storm on his last voyage to Rome so that "neither sun nor stars in many days appeared" (Acts 27:20)? Where is the Lord Jesus Christ called "the bright and morning star" (Rev. 22:16)? Who shall "shine as the brightness of the firmament" and "as the stars for ever and ever" (Dan. 12:3)? Answers to these and other questions appear in the following pages, as well as a complete list of biblical references to astronomical objects.

There has been a sense of hostility between the devotees of science and of the Scriptures. Students of science often distrust the Bible; students of the Bible often distrust science. Yet many people are genuinely interested in both subjects. The following pages are a contribution to an understanding of both subjects. Hostility between students of science and the Scriptures should be dispelled because the same God who created the universe inspired the Scriptures. There is a great spiritual benefit in recognizing the hand of God in creation and in the Scriptures. The stars speak volumes to those who will listen. As the Scriptures speak of the God of the stars, so the stars, to the reverent mind, speak eloquently of the God of the Scriptures. Their message reinforces, rather than threatens, true belief.

BEHOLD THE HEIGHT OF THE STARS,
HOW HIGH THEY ARE!

JOB 22:12

HOW BIG IS OUTER SPACE?

Almost every man at some time in his life has looked up at the stars and pondered the size of the universe. Pascal once said, "The eternal silence of these infinite spaces terrifies me." Man, however, has not had a good estimate of the immense size of the universe until modern astronomical investigations began to reveal the staggering distances between the stars and the almost endless distances of galactic space. Photographic investigations have shown galaxies spread out to almost unbelievable distances and no observable edge of the universe anywhere.

Eliphaz exclaims, "Behold the height of the stars, how high they are!" and Elihu urges Job to "stand still, and consider the wondrous works of God" (Job 22:12; 37:14).

It is common to speak of "empty space," but space is far from empty. Throughout space are gases spread extremely thin— about 16 molecules for each cubic inch of space. This density is actually a much more complete vacuum than any that scientists can create in their laboratories. When one considers the number of cubic inches in space, however, it is apparent that there exists in space a huge quantity of gas. There are also many dust particles scattered throughout the universe. These particles have an obscuring effect that inhibits scientific investigation. There are so many stars in space that the night sky could show solid stars from horizon to horizon. The fact that we see mostly dark sky shows the immense effect of all this dust and gas in space.

There is also radiation in space. The entire electromagnetic spectrum of radiation from the cosmic rays to radio waves constantly irradiates outer space. That spectrum includes cosmic rays, gamma rays, X-rays, ultraviolet rays, visible light rays, infrared rays, heat waves, spark discharges, micro waves, short waves, broadcast radio waves, and long radio waves. These electromagnetic charges do not occupy any physical space, but they are all continually passing through space.

The object nearest to us in outer space is the moon. At an average distance of 238,857 miles away, it has already begun to be explored by man. The next stage of space

exploration, the planets, will be much more difficult because of the greater distances involved. The sun cannot be explored directly because the temperatures are enough to vaporize any spaceship that comes near it. The nearer planets, however, are likely prospects for exploration. The planet Venus comes within 26 million miles of the earth, and the planet Mars within 48 million.

The moon at fourteen days

Although Venus comes closer to Earth than Mars, it is a less promising place because of its high surface temperature, estimated to be 800° Fahrenheit. Reaching the farther planets will be more difficult. Jupiter never comes any nearer than 390 million miles to the earth; Saturn at its closest is 793 million miles away. Conventionally propelled spacecraft could take 987 days to reach Jupiter and 2,043 days to reach Saturn. Obviously, men will need to invent a much more economical high-speed fuel before serious exploration of these planets is possible.

When we lift our eyes from the planets to the stars, we have an entirely different problem: it is not just difficult; it is presently impossible to explore the stars. To illustrate, let us mention only the closest star to our own sun. Located in the constellation Centaurus, it is visible only from the equator southward. This famous star, Alpha Centauri, is 4.326 light-years away. The light we see in that star is actually produced by a group of stars. Alpha Centauri is the principal one. The closest star to us is Proxima Centauri, at a distance of 4.264 light-years. Most authorities believe that Proxima Centauri and the others are related to one another—perhaps in the manner of double stars. Although they are so far from the earth that they appear as one star, they are not to be identified as one star. Even if we could travel at the speed of light—186,000 miles a second—we would still need 4.262 years to reach Proxima Centauri. It would take generations for a rocket ship to reach this star by our present propulsion systems. Other stars would take even longer to reach. Thus, interstellar travel is not now possible.

If we could shrink the size of the stars to pinheads, the relative distance between our sun and Proxima Centauri would still be 100 miles! We never hear of stars colliding; they are so far apart that such collisions are extremely rare. Two pinheads are not likely to collide when they are 100 miles away from one another. The star Arcturus is about 37 light-years from us; the star Spica is over 200 light-years away. The brightest star of Cygnus, Deneb, is about 1,500 light-years from us. These stars are part of just the Milky Way Galaxy.

Our galaxy has a diameter of almost 100,000 light-years, and beyond our Milky Way Galaxy are other galaxies. The nearest ones, the Local Group, include about 20 galaxies.

Our Milky Way Galaxy is on one end of this group; at the other end is the famous M 31 "Andromeda" galaxy (catalogued by Charles Messier in 1771 and subsequently identified as Messier 31, or M 31 for short). It is about twice the size of our Milky Way Galaxy—at least 180,000 light-years in diameter. It is 2,200,000 light-years away from us. Its vast distance made earlier astronomers think it closer to our own size, but now it is recognized to be much larger.

Another member of the Local Group, located just below the constellation Andromeda in Triangulum, is M 33. Astronomers

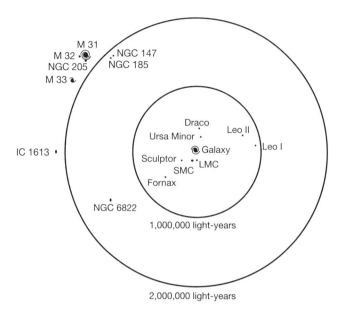

M 31
M 32
NGC 205
M 33

NGC 147
NGC 185

Draco
Ursa Minor
Leo II
Galaxy
Leo I
Sculptor
LMC
SMC
Fornax

IC 1613

NGC 6822

1,000,000 light-years

2,000,000 light-years

The Local Group

estimate that M 33 is 2,400,000 light-years away from us. Still, it is part of the Local Group! Beyond the Local Group, the distances to other galaxies are even greater.

There are apparently hundreds of billions of other galaxies beyond the Local Group. Many of these galaxies are in groups of their own. One such group is a cluster of galaxies in the constellation Coma Berenices. Astronomers estimate that this group of galaxies is about 40 million light-years away from us. The farther our instruments reach out into space, the more such galaxies we can see. We have come nowhere near any observable edge of the universe.

An interesting characteristic of the galaxies is the so-called red shift that those outside our Local Group manifest. When astronomers record the spectrum from these galaxies, the lines in the spectrum are all shifted toward the red end of the spectrum. This shift means that the galaxies are moving away from us. Stranger yet is the fact that the farther a galaxy is from us, the

Cluster of galaxies in Coma Berenices

faster it is moving away from us. Astronomers can line up galaxies in the relative order of their distances from us, and in every case the lines in the spectrum are shifted farther toward the red the farther away the galaxy is. At a distance of 350 million light-years, the lines are shifted a great part of the spectrum.

Even the most distant galaxies do not mark the end of outer space. The farthest objects that astronomers have discovered are the quasi-stellar objects, called "quasars" for short. They were discovered with the help of radio telescopes, because they are all tremendous radio transmitters. The first to be discovered was 3C 48, which appears near the constellation Triangulum. The quasars have more energy than a galaxy, some of it the intense kind known to astronomers as synchrotron radiation; but through a telescope they look no bigger than normally hot stars. This circumstance presents a number of puzzles. Most astronomers now think that the quasars are extremely far away from us—they estimate about five billion light-years. The great red shift that they manifest shows that they are traveling away from us at great speeds—some as much as 80% of the speed of light. If some are traveling as fast as the speed of light, we could never know about it, because they would be traveling too fast for their light to reach us. Needless to say, intensive research is going on to determine more accurately what these strange objects are. No doubt some of the opinions expressed by astronomers today will have to be revised as information increases.

Quasars 3C 48, 3C 273

Now we understand what the prophet Isaiah meant when he spoke of God "Who hath measured the waters in the hollow of his hand, and meted out heaven with the span, and comprehended the dust of the earth in a measure. . . . All nations before him are as nothing; and they are counted to him less than nothing, and vanity. . . . Have ye not known? have ye not heard? hath it not been told you from the beginning? have ye not understood from the foundations of the earth? It is he that sitteth upon the circle of the earth, and the inhabitants thereof are as grasshoppers; that stretcheth out the heavens as a curtain, and spreadeth them out as a tent to dwell in. . . . To whom then will ye liken me, or shall I be equal? saith the Holy One. Lift up your eyes on high, and behold who hath created these things, that bringeth out their host by number: he calleth them all by names by the greatness of his might, for that he is strong in power; not one faileth. . . . Hast thou not known? hast thou not heard, that the everlasting God, the Lord, the Creator of the ends of the earth, fainteth not, neither is weary? there is no searching of his understanding" (Isa. 40:12, 17, 21-22, 25-26, 28).

We think of those words by the psalmist, "What is man, that thou art mindful of him?" (Ps. 8:4). Our God has created a universe so immense that it leaves us speechless. Surely He could ignore this tiny planet on which we live. Yet God is not only powerful enough to create this vast universe, but also loving enough to send His only begotten Son into this world to die for our sins.

THE LION OF THE TRIBE OF JUDA

REVELATION 5:5

North

Cepheus

Cassiopeia

Andromeda

Lyra

Perseus

Ursa Minor

Draco

Auriga

Hercules

Lynx

Corona

Taurus

Boötes

Canes V.

Ursa Major

East

West

Serpens

Leo Minor

Gemini

Orion

Coma B.

Cancer

Canis Minor

Leo

Virgo

Monoceros

Libra

Hydra

Canis Major

Corvus

Crater

Centaurus

Puppis

Vela

South

Stars of spring

THE LION:
THE STARS OF SPRING

Writers have vied with one another in finding words eloquent enough to describe the night skies. Dryden called the stars "the gems of heaven that gild night's sable throne." Carlyle spoke of the "eternal fields of light." Lord Byron termed the stars "the poetry of heaven." Longfellow called them the "forget-me-nots of the angels." Shakespeare referred to them as "these blessed candles of the night" and saw the night sky as "the floor of heaven . . . thick inlaid with patens of bright gold."

Constellations are simply groups of stars that men have thought of as forming figures in the night sky. They are still useful to modern astronomers, for just as knowing that a certain place is in Oregon helps us to find it on a map, knowing that a certain star is in Leo the Lion helps us to find it in the night sky. Although modern astronomers recognize 88 constellations, the ancient astronomers described only 48. Most modern constellations are small and obscure because they only fill in the gaps between the older, better-known constellations.

The original set of 48 constellations is ancient indeed. The Alexandrian astronomer, Ptolemy, drew up a catalog of stars in A.D. 137 in which he described 48 constellations, but the earliest complete description of the 48 constellations is in the poem *Phaenomina* by Aratus, which was written about 270 B.C. The Apostle Paul quotes from this poem in his sermon on Mars' Hill in Athens: God has providentially dealt with mankind "that they should seek the Lord, if haply they might feel after him, and find him, though he be not far from every one of us: For in him we live, and move, and have our being; as certain also of your own poets have said, For we are also his offspring" (Acts 17:27-28).

Clearly, Paul was quite familiar with Aratus's poem on the constellations.

Aratus, however, did not discover the constellations. As early as 1000 B.C. Homer could refer to these constellations as well-known and needing no explanation. Odysseus, observing the starry skies as he sets sail,

> There view'd the Pleiades and the Northern Team,
> And great Orion's more refulgent beam,
> To which around the axle of the sky
> The Bear, revolving, points his golden eye.

In the Egyptian and Babylonian records, references to the constellations go back much further still.

Just how much then did the ancients know about astronomy? In the matter of observational astronomy, modern man is in for a surprise, for the peoples of ancient times made very precise observations of the rising and setting of the sun, moon, and stars. The famous Stonehenge on the Salisbury Plain in England is now recognized as a primitive astronomical observatory. It has long been known that a person standing in the center of that ring of huge stones on Midsummer Day, June 21, would see the sun rise directly over the "heel stone." Recently astronomers have shown that there are 24 perfect alignments between those great stones and the rising and setting of the sun and moon. These alignments could not possibly be accidental. When one remembers that archaeologists date the founding of Stonehenge about 2000 B.C., then one realizes that ancient man was a most careful observer. It is well known that the pyramids in Egypt are laid out in exact orientation with the four cardinal directions—north, east, south, and west. But it is not as well known that practically every temple in ancient Egypt had its main axis lined up with the rising or setting of the sun or of one of the prominent stars such as Canopus or Sirius.

The largest temple ever built, the great temple of Amen-Ra in Karnak, Egypt, is a classic example of this construction. The

Stonehenge

central axis of this temple was kept open throughout all its almost 500-yard length. The temple extended for almost five football fields, past pylon after pylon, gate after gate, colonnade after colonnade. Each gate was smaller than the preceding one. The series of gates acted like diaphragms, shutting out extraneous light. On Midsummer Day the setting sun would flash down the 500-yard length of the temple for just two minutes to illuminate the image of the god on the back wall of the innermost sanctuary.

With so precise a timing device, the ancient priests could calculate the length of the year down to the last second. Since the priests were expected to prophesy the time that the Nile would overflow its banks, this ingenious construction gave them immense power, for the Nile overflows soon after Midsummer Day. Since the agricultural calendar that the rest of the Egyptians followed was not nearly so accurate, the priests sometimes wielded more power than the pharaoh. The great temple of Amen-Ra at Karnak was begun in the eighteenth dynasty soon after 1555 B.C. However, archaeologists have good evidence that

Temple of Amen-Ra, Karnak

20

there was a temple of Amen at Karnak even in the days of the Old Kingdom that began in 2780 B.C. Careful observation of the heavenly bodies is ancient indeed.

One of the most beautiful seasons of the year is spring, and indeed the skies of spring are awesome. It is in the spring that we can view some of the most ancient and interesting constellations. The most famous of the spring constellations is Leo the Lion. A sickle shape of stars forms the head and mane of the Lion to the west. The bright star at the base of the sickle is Regulus, often called the "heart of the Lion." The bright star at the eastern end of the constellation is Denebola, the Lion's tail.

Leo is one of the most ancient and important of all the constellations. In ancient times Leo marked the summer solstice; that is, the sun was in Leo when it reached its greatest elevation in midsummer. This made Leo a very regal constellation, just as the lion is the king of beasts.

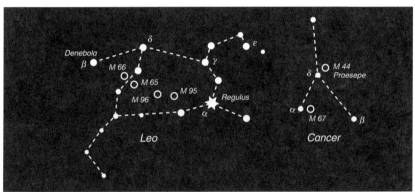

Leo the Lion, Cancer the Crab

Leo is also one of the 12 constellations of the zodiac. The zodiac is that band of sky through which the sun, moon, and planets travel in their apparent path around the earth. The center of the zodiac is the path of the sun, which is called the ecliptic, because all eclipses of the sun and moon occur on that path.

The most important point on the ecliptic has always been the spring equinox. This is the point against the background of the stars at which the sun crosses the equator on its journey to the north about March 21. The problem about this point, however, is that it keeps moving along the ecliptic. The earth is like a giant spinning top, but the gravitational pulls of the sun and moon give the earth a slight wobble. The earth would take about 25,800 years to complete one such wobble. The result of this movement is what is called the precession of the equinox: the spring equinox keeps moving toward the west. At the present time the spring equinox is in the constellation Pisces the Fish, which is below the horizon in the spring. But in the days of Aratus the spring equinox fell in the constellation of Aries the Ram, which now sets in the west very near the horizon. The period of time A.D. 100 back to 2100 B.C. is often called the Age of the Ram because the spring equinox fell in Aries. Even today we have the expression "the first of Aries" meaning the start of spring, although Aries no longer marks this beginning.

Taurus the Bull is immediately to the east of Aries. It is easily recognized by its **V** shape of stars. Throughout the Age of the Ram writers refer to the Bull as marking the beginning of spring. The Roman poet Virgil in the first of his *Georgics* speaks

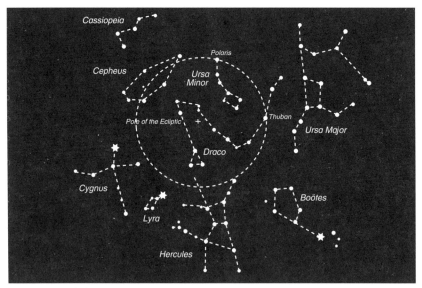

Precession of the equinox

of the coming of spring as the time "when the shining Bull opens the year with gilded horns." The spring equinox fell in Taurus the Bull from 4300 B.C. to 2100 B.C. During this period, called the Age of the Bull, most of the 48 ancient constellations were named and important observations of the heavenly bodies were made.

Thus, in the Age of the Bull, Taurus the Bull stood at the beginning of spring and Leo the Lion marked the beginning of summer. In autumn Scorpius the Scorpion seized the sun, and in winter Aquarius the Water Pourer poured forth the wet months of the year. This arrangement gave importance to what ancient astronomers called the four "royal stars." In Taurus the bright Aldebaran marked the flaming eye of the Bull; in Leo, Regulus shone as the heart of the lion; in Scorpius the bright Antares lit up the body; and near Aquarius the star Fomalhaut marked the mouth of Pisces Austrinus, the Southern Fish, into which Aquarius poured water.

Another result of the wobble of the spinning earth is that the North Pole seems to move among the northern stars. At the present time the axis of the earth's spin is pointed near Polaris,

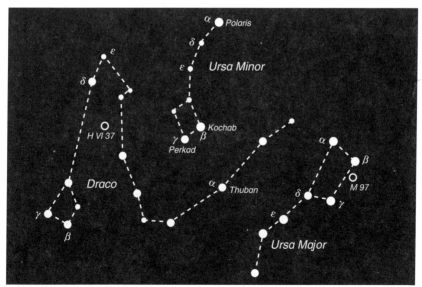

Draco, Ursa Minor, Ursa Major

the so-called North Star. Polaris marks the end of the handle of the Little Dipper in the constellation that astronomers call the Little Bear, or Ursa Minor. Quite close is the Big Dipper in the constellation Ursa Major, the Great Bear. Between the two Dippers snakes the constellation Draco the Dragon, which seems to coil around the Little Dipper.

The earth's wobble means that the pole of the ecliptic traces out a great circle through the northern stars. The pole now points toward Polaris, but back in the year 3000 B.C. the star Thuban was the pole star. Thuban is called by astronomers Alpha Draconis because it is in the constellation Draco the Dragon. The pole is making a complete circuit of the northern stars, but it will take about 25,800 years for the pole to get back to Polaris in the Little Dipper. In our lifetime Polaris will always be the North Star.

Thuban, the Dragon star, was very famous in ancient times. When the Great Pyramid of Giza in Egypt was built about 2900 B.C., the main descending passageway pointed directly at Thuban, which was about three-and-a-half degrees below the pole at that time.

E. Walter Maunder, the former head of the Greenwich Observatory in England, made some interesting calculations about the 48 ancient constellations in relation to Thuban. These constellations cover the sky with the exception of the southern stars, for the southern stars were below the horizon for ancient observers. Maunder calculated that the center of this blank area in the south was the South Pole of the ecliptic in 2700 B.C. This South Pole was almost exactly opposite Thuban when it was the North Pole star. Thus the 48 ancient constellations were probably named as early as 2700 B.C. when Thuban was the pole star.

Of course, the constellations of the zodiac are the oldest of them all and may go back well beyond 3000 B.C. There is an interesting tradition in ancient Egypt concerning Gemini the Twins, the constellation alongside Taurus the Bull. The two brightest stars of Gemini are Castor and Pollux. Before the year 4300 B.C., the spring equinox would have fallen in the constellation of Gemini the Twins. In the Egyptian temple of Dendera, which dates only from the Hellenistic Period, archaeologists found a circular zodiac that embodies a very ancient tradition. Taurus the Bull is pictured as off-center, and the spring equinox is marked by Gemini the Twins. If this tradition be true, the Egyptians were observing the stars before 4300 B.C. Of course, this date goes back beyond recorded history, and such traditions cannot be proved.

Coming back to the Big Dipper, if we extend the arc formed by the stars of the handle, we will come to one of the brightest stars in the sky, Arcturus, in the constellation Boötes the Herdsman. The stars of Boötes form the shape of a great kite. The name Arcturus is a very ancient one; it comes from two Greek words meaning "bear guard." Since this star follows the Great Bear around the pole, Arcturus is an appropriate name. The star Arcturus is about 36 light-years away from us; that is,

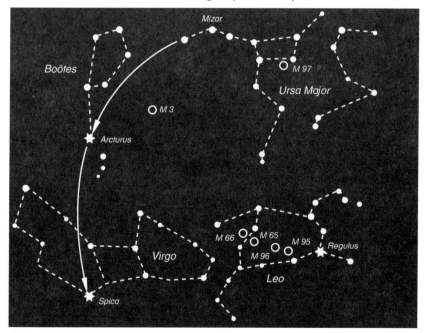

Ursa Major, Boötes, Virgo, Leo

its light takes 36 years to reach us. Because of this time lapse, the light from Arcturus that was used to light up the Chicago World's Fair in 1933 was thought to have left the star during the Columbian Exposition back in the 1890s. Arcturus is moving within our galaxy with a velocity of 75 miles a second. In comparison, our sun is moving with a velocity of 12 miles a second. To put that in familiar terms, the speed of Arcturus, 75 miles a second, is 270,000 miles per hour. Arcturus is really moving!

If we extend this arc beyond Arcturus, we will find the star Spica, the brightest star of the constellation Virgo the Virgin. Spica is more than 200 light-years away; the light we now see coming from Spica left the star before the American Revolutionary War. It gives one a strange feeling to consider that when the light left this star, George Washington, Benjamin Franklin, Thomas Jefferson, and the other founding fathers of our nation were walking this earth.

The stars of this very ancient constellation of the zodiac have a rather large and irregular shape. The Hebrew name for the constellation was Bethulah, which means "virgin"; the name for the star Spica means "a spike or stalk of grain." The Hebrew name for it is Tsemach, which means "branch." This word *tsemach* is the same word that figures so largely in Old Testament prophecy as the name for the Messiah. Although there are many different Hebrew words that mean "branch," this one always refers to the Messiah. The prophet Jeremiah says, "Behold, the days come, saith the Lord, that I will raise unto David a righteous Branch, and a King shall reign and prosper" (Jer. 23:5). It is interesting that the two biblical subjects of the virgin and the branch are combined in this constellation.

Alongside Virgo is Leo the Lion, which reminds us of the Lord Jesus Christ, the Lion of the tribe of Judah, the only rightful heir to the throne of David. Right below Leo is Hydra, the great Water Serpent. Hydra extends for over 100° below Leo and below Virgo. Thus, we have the serpent here as well.

Next to Leo is another constellation of the zodiac, Cancer the Crab. Cancer is the faintest of the zodiac constellations. Near the center of the Crab is the famous star cluster Praesepe, the Beehive. On very clear evenings it can be seen as a faint, hazy patch of light.

Another interesting combination of constellations in the northern sky includes Draco the Dragon, which coils around the Little Dipper and curves back on itself, ending in a group of four stars that mark the head of the Dragon. Alongside Draco is Hercules, named after the hero of Greek mythology. Hercules is easily identified by a keystone shape of stars, but it actually extends over a large area. When Aratus spoke of this constellation, he called it "the One who kneels." Even in Aratus's time no one knew what the kneeling figure represented. Even more strangely, the Kneeler was always pictured with his head toward the south. The star representing the head is Ras Algethi, "head of the kneeler." Thus the figure was kneeling with his heel very close to the head of Draco the Dragon. Alongside the Kneeler is the constellation Serpens the Serpent, which covers a wide area of the sky and is stretching forth its head to seize the Northern Crown, Corona Borealis. But even as the Serpent reaches for the symbol of authority, the Kneeler raises a mighty club with which to crush the head of the Serpent. The bright star near the head of Serpens is called Kornephoros, "club bearer." Is this accidental that the kneeling figure is portrayed as crushing the head of the Serpent, or does this represent a very ancient prophecy? Who knows what Enoch or Noah taught about the Lord's statement to the serpent: "I will put enmity between thee and the woman, and between thy seed and her seed; it shall bruise thy head, and thou shalt bruise his heel" (Gen. 3:15)? It would not be strange if, before any part of the Bible was recorded, the ancient patriarchs found in the constellations signs to embody their oldest truths.

There is probably a reference to Draco the Dragon in the Book of Job. Job says of God, "By his spirit he hath garnished the heavens; his hand hath formed the crooked serpent" (Job 26:13). The Hebrew parallelism means that God has adorned the heavens by the form of the crooked serpent. Isaiah prophesies the Lord's triumph over the serpent. "In that day the Lord with his sore and great and strong sword shall punish leviathan the piercing serpent, even leviathan that crooked serpent; and he shall slay the dragon that is in the sea" (Isa. 27:1). Since the sea is the prophetic symbol of the nations, the prophet is saying that the serpent in the sky is the symbol of the dragon at work in the nations of the world.

Far to the south appears Scorpius the Scorpion. This is one constellation that really looks like its namesake. It is possible to see the claws of the Scorpion and the body with its long curving tail ending in a sharp stinger. The name of the northern star, pointing to Serpens, is Lesath, "the stinger." Antares, the bright red star in the body, is another of the four "royal stars." It is one of the largest stars known, hundreds of times larger than our own sun.

The meanings of these names—Taurus the Bull, Leo the Lion, Virgo the Virgin, and so forth—are dimmed by the passing of the ages. The meanings of some were obscure thousands of years ago. We should be thankful that we are not dependent on signs in the heavens, for we have revelation much more certain than these signs could ever be. God has given to us His infallible Word, the Bible, in order to reveal to us His great love. The constellations will pass away some day, but His Word will not: "Heaven and earth shall pass away, but my words shall not pass away" (Matt. 24:35). All the stars and constellations overhead are simply a manifestation of His glory. "For of him, and through him, and to him, are all things: to whom be glory for ever. Amen" (Rom. 11:36).

[HE] MAKES THE BEAR, ORION, AND THE PLEIADES

JOB 9:9 NASV

North

East

West

South

Andromeda

Cassiopeia

Lacerta

Cepheus

Ursa Minor

Lynx

Ursa Major

Leo Minor

Draco

Pegasus

Cygnus

Canes V.

Leo

Lyra

Coma B.

Delphinus

Sagitta

Hercules

Boötes

Aquarius

Corona

Aquila

Serpens

Virgo

Corvus

Capricornus

Scutum

Ophiuchus

Serpens

Libra

Hydra

Sagittarius

Scorpius

Centaurus

Lupus

Stars of summer

THE CLOCK IN THE SKY:
THE STARS OF SUMMER

Let us imagine ourselves on a Judean hilltop with the boy David when alone with his father's flock he sat looking up as the twilight deepened into the splendor of an oriental sky. As we sit here on the hilltop, the hurry and rush of our modern life is gone; the stars have no competition from bright city lights, and there are no factories pouring forth smoke to obscure our vision.

Over in the north are the seven famous stars of the familiar Big Dipper. The old Arabian astronomers gave them the names that they are known by today: Dubhe, Merak, Phecda, Megrez, Alioth, Mizar, and Alkaid. The Big Dipper is an asterism, that is, a part of a larger group of stars, the constellation Ursa Major, the Great Bear. This constellation is mentioned in the Bible. In order to reveal to Job his human inadequacy, the Lord asks him, among other things, "Can you lead forth [the Mazzaroth] in its season or can you guide the Bear with her [train]?" (Job 38:32 NASV). The power of the Lord does indeed guide the Great Bear in her circuit around the North Pole. In this day of blatant unbelief we need to remember that the Scriptures clearly teach that God is the Creator "who makes the Bear, Orion, and the Pleiades, and the chambers of the south" (Job 9:9 NASV). The rival speculative theories on the origin of the universe are a poor substitute for intelligent faith in the revealed Word of God.

A cluster of faint stars marks the Bear's head. His back stretches over the Dipper's bowl, and the Dipper's handle forms a long tail on the Great Bear. Before Columbus came, the American Indians knew bears well enough to know that they had short tails, and though they, like their European neighbors, saw a Great Bear in the sky, they imagined that the three stars in the Dipper's handle were three Indians who followed the Great Bear. The first Indian had a bow and arrow with which to kill the Bear; the second Indian carried a pot in which to cook the bear meat; and the third Indian carried firewood. With close observation we can see the pot that the second Indian carries; for the second star, Mizar, has a tiny star, Alcor, right alongside it. The Arabians had an expression, "He can see Alcor," meaning a person has good eyesight. We would say, "He has 20/20 vision."

The Big Dipper is an important group, especially to those who use the stars to find their way. With it we can locate Polaris, the North Star, situated almost directly above the North Pole of the earth. The two stars forming the front of the bowl of the Big Dipper, Dubhe and Merak (Dubhe marks the lip of the Dipper, and Merak the bottom corner), are the pointers. If we draw a line from Merak through Dubhe and extend the line, we come to Polaris, which is not particularly bright but very conveniently placed. Since Polaris lies almost directly above the North Pole, we can draw a line from Polaris straight down to the horizon in order to find north as a direction on the horizon. This is a much truer north than any we can determine using a magnetic compass, because geographic north and magnetic north do not generally coincide. If we can identify the North Star, we can be very sure of our directions.

Now let us use the Big Dipper as a key in order to find other constellations in the sky. The line formed by the two stars at the rear of the Dipper's bowl, Megrez and Phecda, can be extended toward the west in order to locate the bright star Regulus, the heart of Leo the Lion. If we think of the handle of the Big Dipper as the arc of a circle, and extend this arc southward, we come to the star Arcturus, the brightest star of the constellation Boötes the Herdsman. Extending the arc still further south to the next very bright star, we find Spica, the brightest star of the constellation Virgo the Virgin. Then to the north between the Big

Dipper and the Little Dipper is the most famous of the serpent constellations, Draco the Dragon. And under the curving handle of the Big Dipper is a dark area of the sky that contains the constellation Canes Venatici, the Hunting Dogs.

The most fascinating feature of the Big Dipper is that it forms with the North Star a great clock in the sky by which one can tell what time it is in any given month in the year. Let us see how it works. Polaris, the North Star, is the center of the clock dial. The pointers, Dubhe and Merak, the two stars at the front of the bowl of the Big Dipper, form the hour hand. Although there are no numbers on the dial and no minute hand, we can still tell time quite accurately. In the month of May at 9:00 P.M. the pointers are at the 11:00 position. Thirty days later in the month of June at 9:00 P.M. the pointers will have moved over to the 10:00 position. In any one evening the pointers take about two hours to move one hour's space on the clock dial. So at 11:00 P.M. in May the pointers will also be at the 10:00 spot. At 1:00 A.M. in May the pointers will be at the 9:00 position. This 9:00 position indicates an actual 9:00 P.M. in the month of July.

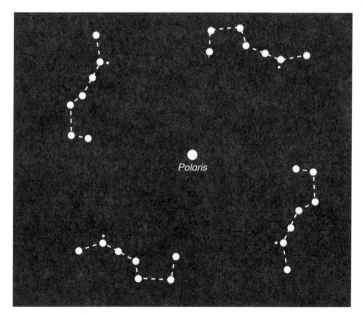

The Big Dipper clock

33

In July the skies look much different from the way they looked in the spring. Leo the Lion is setting far over in the west. The constellations Boötes and Virgo have moved correspondingly toward the west. Sagittarius the Archer, another constellation of the zodiac, is now in view in the south. The bow has a very oriental shape to it, and the arrow is pointed straight at the Scorpion. Above the Archer is a diamond shape of stars that marks the wings of Aquila the Eagle, the brightest star of which is Altair.

High over Aquila is the small constellation Lyra the Lyre with the brightest star of the summer skies, Vega. Lyra is famous as

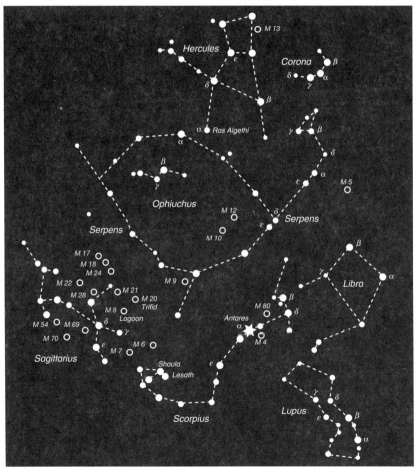

Sagittarius, Scorpius, and vicinity

34

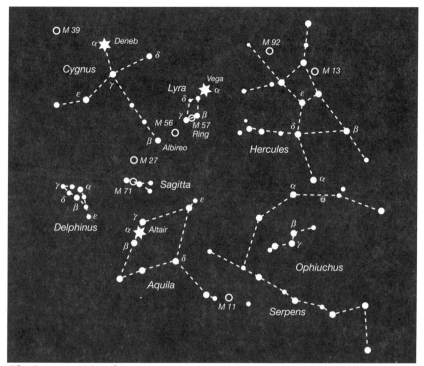

The Summer Triangle

the location of a cloud of dust and gas called the Ring Nebula. Alongside Lyra is the constellation Cygnus the Swan with its brightest star, Deneb. Cygnus is often called the Northern Cross because its shape is certainly that of a cross. The three bright stars, Deneb, Vega, and Altair, are called the Summer Triangle.

If we trace an imaginary line between Vega and Arcturus, we can find two other constellations of the summer skies. Right alongside Boötes is the beautiful Corona Borealis, the Northern Crown. Between Corona and Vega is the keystone shape of stars in the constellation Hercules. It forms a great **K** in the sky.

Directly to the south is one of the most dramatic of all the constellations, Scorpius the Scorpion. The brightest star of Scorpius is Antares, which means "the Rival of Mars." Antares, a giant red star, looks like the red planet Mars. When the two are in the same part of the sky, they do indeed rival one another.

Mars is the brighter of the two in appearance, but only because the planets are so close to us. If the star Antares were as close to us as Mars, we would be engulfed in its flaming interior. In fact, Antares is estimated to be 320 times larger than our sun, so that if it were placed where our sun is, the diameter of Antares would extend out beyond the orbit of earth and far beyond the orbit of Mars.

In front of the Scorpion is a faint constellation, Libra the Scales. The ancient world knew it as the Claws of the Scorpion. Above the Scorpion is the constellation Ophiuchus the Serpent Holder. It is a large group of stars that portrays a man gripping a serpent, the constellation Serpens. Serpens rears its head up to seize the Northern Crown and extends its tail all the way to Aquila the Eagle. Below the Scorpion is the small constellation Lupus the Wolf.

During August, the pointers of our clock at 9:00 P.M. are at the 8:00 position. The stars of summer are moving into the west and will soon be replaced by the stars of autumn. When the pointers pass the 7:00 position, we will be in September. The fall is the most difficult time of year in which to see the Big Dipper. The reason for that is quite apparent. In October the pointers at 9:00 P.M. are in the 6:00 position and the horizon light obscures most of the constellation. When the pointers reach 5:00, it is November, and at the 4:00 position the pointers indicate December. When the pointers reach the 3:00 position, the Dipper is standing on its handle, and we are in the month of January. As the pointers approach the 2:00 position of February, the harbinger of spring, the sickle of Leo the Lion, is rising in the east. When the pointers reach the 1:00 position in March, the great Orion is setting in the west, and Leo the Lion is rising higher in the sky.

In March we can follow the handle of the Big Dipper to Arcturus in the constellation Boötes, which comes up in the east. When the pointers at 9:00 P.M. come to the 12:00 position, we are in April, and the spring stars are very much in evidence. Leo is at the zenith, and by following the handle of the Dipper past Arcturus, we can find Spica in the constellation Virgo the Virgin coming into view. In May when the pointers pass the 11:00 position, we have made a complete circuit on the dial of our great clock.

The changing seasons lead naturally to a consideration of why there are different seasons and why the temperature and weather are so radically different in each season. The axis of our earth is inclined 23½° from the perpendicular of its orbit around the sun. This position means that in midwinter the Northern Hemisphere is pointed away from the sun, and even though it is actually closer to the sun than in mid-summer, the sun's rays are striking the earth's Northern Hemisphere at such an angle that very little heat is getting through the earth's atmosphere. On the other hand, the Southern Hemisphere is pointed toward the sun, and, hence, it is summer south of the equator. Three months later when the earth has moved around to the position of the spring equinox, the sun is directly over the equator, and both hemispheres receive equal heat from the sun. Here in the Northern Hemisphere we enjoy springtime, whereas the people in the Southern Hemisphere experience autumn. Again three months later the earth has moved around to the summer solstice on June 21. At this time the North Pole, pointing toward the sun, brings summer to the Northern Hemisphere because the sun's rays are striking the earth more directly. At the same time the Southern Hemisphere, pointing away from the sun, has its winter. Because the earth is closest to the sun during the northern winter and farthest from it during the northern summer, the Southern Hemisphere has hotter summers and colder winters than the Northern Hemisphere.

The period of time by which all the calendars and seasons are measured is the tropical year, that is, the length of time between two successive returns of the sun to the spring equinox.

Astronomers have measured this period at 365 days, 5 hours, 48 minutes, and 46 seconds. The sidereal year, which is the period of time it takes the sun to return to the same point in relation to the distant stars, is about 20 minutes longer than the tropical year.

The passing seasons remind us of the old Italian proverb, "Man measures time, and time measures man." Man's greatest monuments crumble into dust as the seasons become years, the years become centuries, and the centuries become ages. The psalmist has expressed this well: "As for man, his days are as grass: as a flower of the field, so he flourisheth. For the wind passeth over it, and it is gone; and the place thereof shall know it no more. But the mercy of the Lord is from everlasting to everlasting upon them that fear him, and his righteousness unto children's children" (Ps. 103:15-17). Therefore, the prophet exhorts, "Seek ye the Lord while he may be found, call ye upon him while he is near" (Isa. 55:6).

The contemplation of the wonders of God's creation should awe and humble our minds. But the realization that this same God of the universe has invited us, through the Lord Jesus Christ, to be reconciled to Himself and to dwell with Him throughout all the ages of eternity makes us speechless with wonder. "O the depth of the riches both of the wisdom and knowledge of God! how unsearchable are his judgments, and his ways past finding out!" (Rom. 11:33).

LET THEM BE FOR SIGNS, AND FOR SEASONS,
AND FOR DAYS AND YEARS

GENESIS 1:14

Stars of autumn

THE SIGNS IN THE SKY:
THE STARS OF AUTUMN

From his beginning man has been fascinated by objects in the skies. The sun, moon, planets, and stars have been subjects of study and speculation for millennia. Astronomy is by far the oldest of the sciences. Over 3,000 years ago the ancient Babylonian astronomers were making careful records of their observations of the paths of the planets and the rising and setting of the sun, moon, and stars. Their ancient records, written on clay tablets, have been discovered by archaeologists, and these Babylonian observations look very much like the tables found in a modern nautical almanac.

But it seems to be easy for man to lose himself in a maze of statistical tables and to forget or ignore the God who has created the wonders of the skies. In many educational institutions today one could hear a lecture on the origin of the solar system or even on the origin of the universe with no mention of the name of God. The very first reference in the Bible to these celestial objects puts them in their proper perspective. Genesis 1:16-17 says: "And God made two great lights; the greater light to rule the day, and the lesser light to rule the night: he made the stars also. And God set them in the firmament of the heaven to give light upon the earth." God created the sun, moon, and stars and set the earth in the most beneficial relationship to them.

The Hebrew word *rakeea*, translated *firmament*, really means "expanse" and should not be thought of as denoting something solid, a misinterpretation some liberal theologians try to read into this passage. The word, in fact, gives a graphic picture of space: "And God set them in the expanse of the heaven to give light upon the earth."

Among the first things that one notices in the autumn night sky are the moon and the bright planets, including Mercury, Venus, Mars, Jupiter, and Saturn. The planets and the moon are all spread out roughly along the path of the sun, called the ecliptic. It is easy to see why many of the ancient peoples thought that the sun and planets, as well as the moon, revolved around the earth. Even though the early astronomers observed the backward motion of some of the planets, they had no adequate explanation for such motion until Copernicus advanced his famous heliocentric theory. But thanks to the great telescopes and instruments of modern science, today's astronomers have a much better understanding of the heavens than the ancients had. Now our investigations are reaching out millions of light-years to stars that were invisible to preceding generations. Such stars may shine faintly even in the great telescopes.

In the autumn sky is the very beautiful group of stars known as the Northern Cross. It is an asterism, that is, a part of a large constellation called Cygnus the Swan. Farther over on the western horizon is the constellation Hercules, which can be easily recognized by a keystone shape of stars. Between the two stars

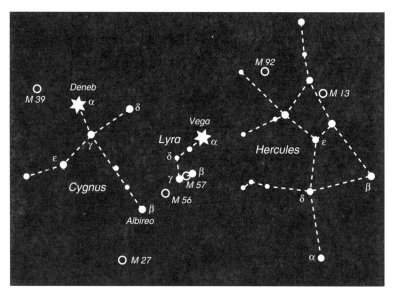

Cygnus, Lyra, Hercules

on the long side of the keystone is a famous star cluster called by astronomers M 13. On very clear evenings it is possible to see this star cluster with the unaided eye as a faint, blurred star. M 13 is a good example of a globular cluster. The stars are packed together so closely in the center that individual stars cannot be discerned. Astronomers estimate that as many as a half million stars are in this cluster. A little more than 100 globular clusters have been discovered by astronomers. They seem to be grouped in a spherical shape around our galaxy, which is a vastly greater group of stars with a flat, pancake-like shape.

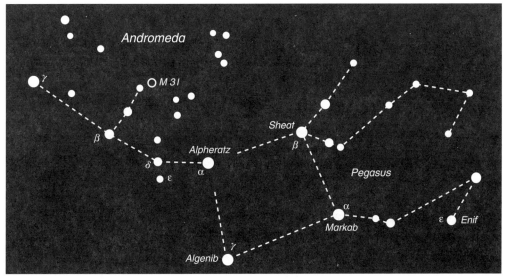

Andromeda, Pegasus

High overhead is the great square of Pegasus. Very few stars are visible within the square, so it is an easy object to spot in the autumn skies. Three stars of the square are in the constellation Pegasus the Flying Horse. They are named Sheat, Markab, and Algenib. The fourth star, Alpheratz, is actually in the constellation Andromeda, which is located to the east. Andromeda is an important constellation for the star observer to remember because in it is the most distant object it is possible to see with the naked eye, the great spiral galaxy M 31.

Between Pegasus and Aquila the Eagle is the small constellation Delphinus the Dolphin, which is made up of a very tiny diamond shape of stars and a small tail. Alongside the Dolphin is the even smaller constellation Sagitta the Arrow. Both of these small constellations were known to the ancient world and were numbered among the 48 constellations. Above Sagitta is a dark area of the sky in which there is not a single star bright enough to be noticed without a telescope. This dark area has been named by modern astronomers Vulpecula the Little Fox. In Vulpecula above the point of the arrow is the Dumbbell nebula, so called because of its apparent shape. It is another planetary nebula. The constellation Equuleus the Horse is just below Delphinus.

Below Andromeda is the tiny constellation Triangulum, formed by a simple triangle of stars. In Triangulum is another beautiful spiral galaxy, M 33. Although this galaxy is not as large as the one in Andromeda, it is fully as beautiful. It is relatively

M 33 in Triangulum

close to our own Milky Way Galaxy. Astronomers call it part of the "Local Group."

Toward the north is Cassiopeia with its famous **W** or **M** shape, depending on the angle of view. Not far from Cassiopeia is the North Star, Polaris, at the end of the handle of the Little Dipper. Very low on the northern horizon and, therefore, difficult to see is the Big Dipper. Draco the Dragon coils around the Little Dipper. Between Cassiopeia and Draco the Dragon is the constellation Cepheus. It is not a very impressive sight, but five main stars form a pentagonal shape.

In considering the northern stars, we may recall Job's observation that God "stretches out the north over empty space, and hangs the earth on nothing" (Job 26:7 NASV). Some expositors treat this verse as though it taught that there is a "hole" among the stars somewhere in the north. This is a misinterpretation of the verse. In the first place modern telescopes have recorded an abundant profusion of stars, even in areas where the naked eye can see nothing, that preceding centuries could not imagine. There is no "hole" among the stars anywhere.

In the second place the verse refers not to the northern part of the sky but to that of the earth, and it proceeds from a part of the earth to the whole. It is a good example of Hebrew parallelism. It really means that God stretches out the north part of the earth over empty space and hangs the whole earth upon nothing; that is, the earth does not rest upon anything, either in part or in whole. This is a striking astronomical truth for a writer to set forth who may have been a contemporary of Abraham.

The immense profusion of stars is most apparent in the Milky Way overhead, which runs through the constellation Cygnus the Swan. In a tiny patch of the Milky Way is the Veil Nebula, which is too small to be seen with the naked eye but which displays vast numbers of stars. In the great telescopes the entire Milky Way can be resolved into individual stars. These billions and billions of stars—along with the planets, moon, and sun—are all grouped together in a great pancake-like shape that astronomers call the Milky Way Galaxy. When we look out through the edge of our galaxy, we look past so many stars that the sky appears milky. When we look out through the flat side of our galaxy, we see fewer stars, but even here a countless number appear through a telescope.

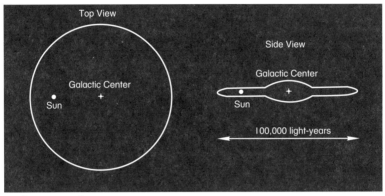

Milky Way Galaxy

Men have named only a few hundred of the brighter, more spectacular stars, and most of these names are from the ancient Arabian and Hebrew astronomers. Men seem to have taken a much greater interest in the stars in those days. The stars today are commonly designated by the letters of the Greek alphabet. The brightest star of a constellation is usually called alpha, the second brightest beta, and so on, until the Greek alphabet is exhausted. The fainter stars are given the letters of the Roman alphabet, and the fainter ones yet are then given numbers. For example, over in the northeast is Perseus, which has the shape of the letter **A** written in a very fancy longhand style. The brightest star of Perseus, Mirfak, is called Alpha Persei; the second bright-est, Algol, is called Beta Persei, and so on through the Greek and Roman alphabets and into the numbers.

Only spectacular stars like Algol are named. Algol comes from an old Arabic name, Al Ghul, meaning "the demon."

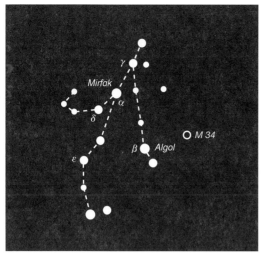

Perseus

Astronomers may have named it this because of its strange behavior. For two days and eleven hours Algol is a second magnitude star; then, mysteriously it dims down in five hours to a third magnitude star; then in another five hours it brightens up to a second magnitude star again. Today we know that Algol is a double star; that is, there are two stars close together but so far away from us that we can see only one. These two stars are revolving around one another. When the dim one passes in front of the bright one, an eclipse occurs, and the light dims down; when the dim star passes away from in front of the bright one, the light increases again.

Unless a star is very bright or very unusual, it does not have a name. But then, most stars are not even numbered. In the great star catalogues that astronomers have made by mapping the sky through telescopes, only a few hundred thousand stars are numbered. There are billions and billions of stars recorded on the photographic plates that are not even numbered, much less named. But the psalmist says that God "telleth the number of the stars; he calleth them all by their names. Great is our Lord, and of great power: his understanding is infinite" (Ps. 147:4-5). Though it is impossible for men to name all the stars, it is certainly possible for God. He who created all the stars has a name for each one.

The first chapter of Genesis indicates that the old names of the stars and constellations may have more significance than we generally attribute to them. "And God said, Let there be lights in the firmament of the heaven to divide the day from the night; and let them be for signs, and for seasons, and for days and years" (Gen. 1:14). Now the Hebrew word *oth,* which is translated "sign" in this verse, occurs 79 times in the Old Testament. Three of those occurrences refer to the ensign or standard of a tribe, but 75 times besides this verse it has a religious significance. Therefore, the presumption is that the word "signs" has a religious significance in this verse as well.

The objects in the sky present many different kinds of signs. The most striking are the comets. The ancients regarded these as portents of grave disaster. Therefore, the prophet Jeremiah exhorts Judah, "Be not dismayed at the signs of heaven; for the heathen are dismayed at them" (Jer. 10:2). One who knows the God who created the heavens need not fear the signs and events in the heavens.

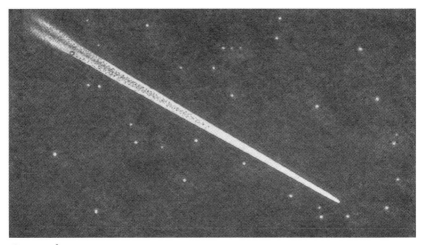

Comet of 1811

One group of signs mentioned in the Bible is a little different from the others. When the Lord answers Job out of the whirlwind, He asks a series of questions in order to bring Job to a realization of his inadequacy. One of the questions is, "Can you lead forth [the Mazzaroth] in its season?" (Job 38:32 NASV).

Merrill Unger interprets Mazzaroth as "the twelve signs of the zodiac."[1]

Four constellations of the zodiac are in their best viewing position in the autumn skies. Over in the south and somewhat toward the west is Capricornus the Horned Goat. Its general shape is a rather irregular triangle. Most of the ancient names of the stars in this constellation refer to some form of goat. The top star in the western corner of Capricornus has the name Gaedi, Arabic for "kid," a young goat. The Hebrew name for it was Gedhi, which also means "kid." The star at the opposite end of the constellation is called Deneb Algedi, which means "the tail of the kid."

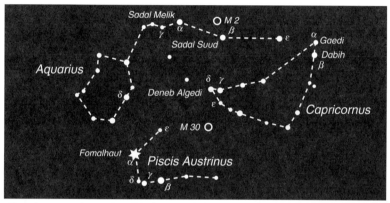

Capricornus, Aquarius, Piscis Austrinis

The next sign of the zodiac is Aquarius the Water Carrier. Aquarius starts above Capricornus and extends eastward to a group of three stars close together; from there it extends down toward the horizon. The group of three stars is called the water jar, and Aquarius is pictured as pouring a great stream of water from the jar on his shoulder. In fact, the Hebrew name for this constellation is Deli, which means "water jar" or "urn."

There is a beneficiary of all this water being poured forth. The very bright star low in the sky is Fomalhaut, one of the southernmost of all first magnitude stars that can be seen from

[1]Merrill F. Unger, *The New Unger's Bible Dictionary*, R. K. Harrison, ed.(Chicago: Moody Press, 1988), 828.

our latitude. Fomalhaut marks the mouth of the Southern Fish, Piscis Austrinus, which is pictured as drinking the water that Aquarius pours forth.

The next constellation in the zodiac is Pisces the Fish. There are really two fish right below the Great Square of Pegasus, but they are always represented as linked together.

The fourth constellation of the zodiac that is visible in autumn is Aries the Ram. Aries is a small constellation with just a few stars bright enough to be seen with the naked eye. The brightest star of the constellation is named Hamal, which is the Arabic word meaning "sheep." The Hebrew word for this constellation is Taleh, which means "young lamb."

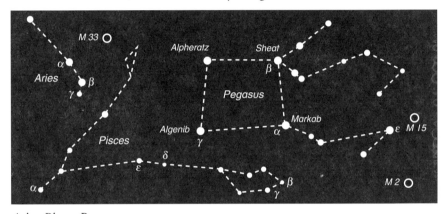

Aries, Pisces, Pegasus

Taken separately these constellations seem not to have much spiritual significance, but together they seem to point to Christ. Capricornus, the goat, reminds us of Christ our sacrifice: the Mosaic law specified "one kid of the goats for a sin offering" (Num. 7:16). Aquarius eternally pouring water reminds us of the passage in which "Jesus stood and cried, saying, If any man thirst, let him come unto me, and drink" (John 7:37). Pisces the Fish reminds us that centuries ago the fish was used by the early church as a symbol of their faith. The Greek word for fish, *ichthus,* is spelled with the same letters as those which comprise

50

the initial letters of the phrase "Jesus Christ, God's Son, Savior." Aries the Ram brings to mind the words of John the Baptist, "Behold the Lamb of God, which taketh away the sin of the world" (John 1:29).

Whatever the spiritual significance these signs may have once had (in many things we truly "see through a glass, darkly"[I Cor. 13:12]), the Lord has given us something more certain than signs in the heavens, more certain than a voice of God speaking from heaven. The Apostle Peter testifies concerning the voice of God which he heard on the Mount of Transfiguration, "This voice which came from heaven we heard, when we were with him in the holy mount." But he adds, "We have also a more sure word of prophecy; whereunto ye do well that ye take heed, as unto a light that shineth in a dark place, until the day dawn, and the day star arise in your hearts" (II Pet. 1:18-19).

SEEK HIM THAT MAKETH THE SEVEN STARS AND ORION

AMOS 5:8

Stars of winter

THE SEVEN STARS AND ORION:
THE STARS OF WINTER

In winter the stars appear their brightest. Not only do the cold, clear winter skies enable one to see the stars more easily, but the stars that are visible then are the brightest and most spectacular of the entire year.

The Bible mentions many of the stars and constellations of the winter skies. "Seek him that maketh the seven stars and Orion," exhorts Amos (5:8). These two groups of stars attract the eye more quickly than any others. The fascinating group of seven stars in the constellation Taurus is called the Pleiades, and high overhead the great constellation Orion dominates the winter sky. The three stars in a straight line are called the Belt of Orion. All three are tremendously bright stars. Since they are at a great distance from us, their apparent brightness is much less than their actual brightness. The star on the eastern side has the Arabic name Alnitak, "the belt." The star on the western end is Mintaka, an Arabic synonym for "belt" or "girdle." The star in the center has the name Alnilam, meaning in Arabic "the string of pearls." This sight makes a spectacular belt! The ancient Chinese called these stars "the three kings," while today modern astronomers often call them the "yardstick" because the line they form is just three degrees long.

The bright star in the lower right corner marking the foot of Orion is named Rigel, Arabic for "foot." Rigel is one of the brightest stars in all the sky in absolute magnitude, but it too is so far away from us that its true brightness is not appreciated. Astronomers have estimated that its actual luminosity is 21,000 times greater than that of our sun.

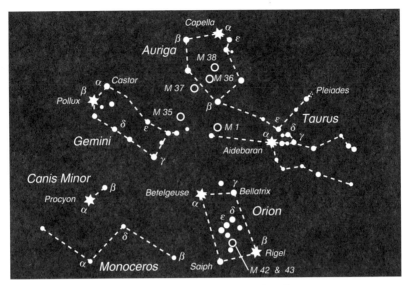

Gemini, Auriga, Taurus, Orion, Monoceros, Canis Minor

The two stars above and to the north of the belt mark the shoulders of Orion: Bellatrix is his left shoulder and Betelgeuse is his right. The meaning of the strange name Betelgeuse is much disputed, but traditionally it refers to the bright jewel on the shoulder of Orion. All the rest of the stars of Orion are white, but Betelgeuse is famous for its reddish hue.

The name of the star straight down from Betelgeuse that completes this quadrilateral is Saiph, which apparently comes from an Arabic word for "sword." Today we usually refer to some faint stars coming down from the belt as the sword. Only the bottom star can be seen easily, but with a pair of binoculars a whole line of stars can be seen. There is a good reason for their faint and hazy appearance. The great cloud nebula in Orion surrounds some of these stars. One of the most beautiful sights that can be seen with the aid of a telescope, this nebula is made up of a cloud of gas spread out to an extreme thinness. Astronomers estimate that there are only a few atoms for each cubic inch of space. No scientist can create a vacuum that rare in the laboratory, and yet this cloud makes up in size what it lacks in density.

The Great Cloud Nebula in Orion

Astronomers use the light-year to measure great distances. Light travels at the speed of 186,000 miles a second; a light-year is the distance light can travel in a whole year. This distance is tremendous. Light can travel the nearly 93 million miles between the sun and our earth in just 8 minutes. But astronomers estimate that this cloud of gas is 160 light-years in diameter; that is, it would take light 160 years to pass from one side of this cloud to the other. So although a considerable volume of gas is in that area, it is spread out so thinly that in any one spot it amounts to a vacuum.

The stars within this cloud, bombarding the gas with ultraviolet radiation, cause the cloud to glow like a fluorescent light. Under the influence of these stars, the gas cloud is glowing by itself as it emits radiation. Only very hot stars can cause a gas cloud to glow by itself.

The constellation Orion seems to have signified a great hunter, a mighty man, or a giant to many of the peoples of ancient times. The Greeks knew Orion as the mighty hunter because Homer in *The Odyssey* in 1000 B.C. called Orion "the mighty hunter." The Arabs called this constellation Al Jabbar, which means "the giant," and the Jews called it Gibbor, meaning "mighty one."

The word translated *Orion* in the Bible occurs four times in an astronomical sense in the Old Testament. The Hebrew word is *kesil,* which means "fool." The biblical fool is not mentally deficient, but impious and ungodly—a rebel against God. "How long, ye simple ones, will ye love simplicity? and the scorners delight in their scorning, and fools hate knowledge?" (Prov. 1:22). In Proverbs as elsewhere the word "fool," *kesil,* refers to one who willfully rejects the knowledge of God.

In the Book of Job, the Lord teaches Job his insufficiency without God. From the whirlwind the Lord asks Job, "Can you bind the chains of the Pleiades, or loose the cords of Orion?" (Job 38:31 NASV). This passage pictures Orion as bound to his place in the sky. Jewish tradition holds that this constellation is to be identified with a specific mighty man, Nimrod. The book of Genesis calls Nimrod a "mighty hunter before the Lord" (Gen.

10:9), and traditionally this early ruler of Babylon arrogated many honors to himself, among them calling this constellation by his own name. But the person who leaves God out of his plans, no matter how shrewd and practical he may be, is still a fool.

The constellation Orion can be used as a key to find the position of a number of other constellations. If we follow the line of the belt stars farther to the west, we come to a **V** shape of stars that marks the face of Taurus the Bull. Aldebaran, the bright red star in the constellation, is much closer to us than the cluster of stars which makes up the **V**. They are called the Hyades. Following the lines of the **V** up in the sky, we come to two stars that are the tips of the Bull's horns. Right alongside the lower star is the position of the Crab Nebula.

When we follow the line of the belt stars beyond the **V** in Taurus, we come to a famous group of seven stars, the Pleiades. It is strange that they are called the Seven Stars, because the average person can see only six stars here, and people with eyesight sharp enough to see seven stars can often see one or two besides that. Scores of visible stars make this cluster one of the

The Pleiades and nebulosity

59

most impressive sights in the skies for viewing with binoculars. The great telescopes have mapped up to 500 stars in this cluster, all moving through space together. There is a good reason for the hazy appearance around these stars: not only are there hundreds and hundreds of stars there, but there are clouds of luminous gas around some of them similar to the Orion Nebula.

The Hebrew name for the Pleiades was Kimah, which means "cluster" or "heap"—a very apt name for this star cluster. Every time the Pleiades are mentioned in the Bible, the constellation Orion is also mentioned, the two of them being the two most remarkable sights of the winter skies. "Canst thou bind the [cluster of the] Pleiades, or loose the bands of Orion?" (Job 38:31). Obviously no man can bind stars into a cluster and make them move through space together. It is, however, a small thing for the Creator of the universe to do.

The Pleiades

The constellation Taurus the Bull figures in the interpretation of a familiar passage of Scripture. When the disobedient Israelites made the golden calf and offered sacrifice to it (Acts 7:41), God "gave them up to worship the host of heaven" (Acts 7:42). The phrase "host of heaven" certainly refers to the astronomical bodies. Scripture adds, "Yea, ye took up the tabernacle of Moloch, and the star of your god Remphan" (Acts 7:43). The Israelites, in making the golden calf, had borrowed the worship of the Egyptian bull god Apis. The golden calf was merely a physical representation of the astronomical deity of Taurus the Bull, just as the Egyptian worship of their god Ra was a worship of the sun. In later years the Israelites would extend their idolatry to worshiping Moloch and other astronomical gods, for which the Lord was to carry them away captive beyond Babylon (Acts 7:43). The worship of the golden calf was the beginning of the idolatrous worship of the whole host of heaven that the prophets so bitterly denounced (Ezek. 8:13-18). The Israelites even became sun worshipers like the Egyptians (Ezek. 8:16).

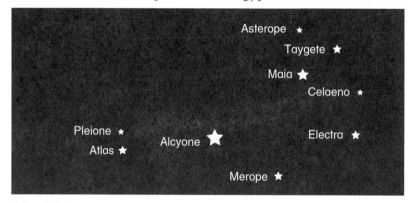

The Pleiades

Using the constellation Orion as a key again, starting with the line of belt stars and going in the opposite direction toward the southeast, we come to the constellation Canis Major, the Great Dog, with its very bright star, Sirius, the brightest star in all the skies. Sirius, the "dog star," gives its name to the "dog days" of summer. The name "dog days" does not mean that it is just too hot for a dog; it signifies that the sun rises at the same time as Sirius, at which time, of course, the hot days of midsummer are upon us. At that time of year Sirius is too close to the sun to be seen.

Sirius is almost a whole magnitude brighter than any other star. The reason is that it is one of the closest stars to us. Astronomers estimate that Sirius is only 8.6 light-years from the earth. This may seem like a tremendous distance (and in our ordinary way of thinking, it is), but other stars are at vastly greater distances from us. The three belt stars in Orion appear less bright than Sirius because they are much farther away—at least 1,500 light-years from us. If they were placed as near as Sirius, they would far outshine Sirius. Still Sirius is not a faint star; astronomers estimate that it is 30 times more luminous than our sun.

Magnitude is an astronomical term for the brightness of a star to earthly view. The so-called first-magnitude stars are the brightest in the sky; in fact, some of them, such as Sirius, are so bright that they have a negative value of brightness. The sixth-magnitude stars are the faintest stars that can be seen with the naked eye. Astronomers have scaled them by equal intervals so that first-magnitude stars are about two and a half times brighter than second-magnitude stars; the second-magnitude stars are two and a half times brighter than third-magnitude stars, and so on. It used to be that the faintest stars that could be detected in the greatest telescopes were classified as twenty-third magnitude stars, but now even fainter ones can be seen. The Apostle Paul refers to this variation in brightness when he says, "There is one glory of the sun, and another glory of the moon, and another glory of the stars: for one star differeth from another star in glory" (I Cor. 15:41). The glories of the heavens only image the preeminent glory of the Lord Jesus Christ, the "bright and morning star" (Rev. 22:16), whose second coming shall usher in the age of peace, for He is the "Prince of Peace" (Isa. 9:6). Without Christ the world cannot have peace, for only righteousness can bring peace.

Coming back to Orion, if we start with Betelgeuse and imagine a line down to Sirius, we have one side of an almost perfect equilateral triangle formed by the star Procyon in the constellation Canis Minor, the Little Dog. The name Procyon means the "one before the dog," and it gets this name because it rises just slightly before Sirius, the great dog star. These three stars—Betelgeuse, Sirius, and Procyon—are known as the Great Winter Triangle.

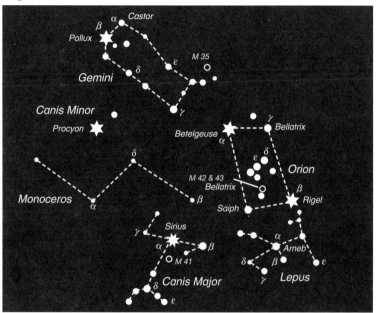

Gemini, Orion, Lepus, Canis Major, Monoceros, Canis Minor

We can use the top line of the Winter Triangle to find yet another constellation. Again starting with Betelgeuse, let us travel along to Procyon, then at Procyon make a right angle, turn, and go up toward the north until we come to the two famous stars Castor and Pollux in the constellation Gemini the Twins. Pollux is the star closest to Procyon, and Castor is beside Pollux. The constellation Gemini is made up of two roughly parallel lines of stars that form two "stick men" in the sky. The star at the end of Castor's line is called Propus, which means "the forward foot."

The two stars Castor and Pollux are mentioned in Acts 28:11. When the Apostle Paul was shipwrecked on the island of Melita (today called Malta), he was compelled to spend the winter there because of stormy seas. After three months, Paul's company "departed in a ship of Alexandria, which had wintered in the isle, whose sign was Castor and Pollux," the twin brothers. It was the custom to paint pictures of the deities on the prows of ships for identification as well as supposed protection. In Roman mythology Castor and Pollux were the patron deities of sailors, and ships commonly bore their picture and name.

Coming back again to Orion, we now go south to a faint group of stars below Orion and alongside Canis Major: the constellation Lepus the Hare. There seems to be grand irony implied in this designation. The only animal that Orion, the mighty hunter, has tracked down is a poor rabbit, the meekest of animals. The brightest star in Lepus is called Arneb, Arabic for "hare" or "rabbit." To the west of Lepus, another faint constellation, Eridanus the River, flows past Orion underneath Taurus and on southward below the southern horizon. Its brightest stars are not visible from northern latitudes.

Auriga, Perseus, Taurus

Going in the opposite direction, straight north from Orion, we come to the irregular oval of stars that is the constellation Auriga. The Latin name Auriga means "charioteer." Its brightest star has the name Capella, which is Latin for "little she-goat." The three fainter stars close to Capella are called "the kids." The ancients had no expla-

64

nation for Auriga's holding a mother goat and her kids. Perhaps the ancient Jewish tradition has the answer. The Jews held that Auriga was a shepherd, and they may have been reminded of those Old Testament passages in which the Lord says, "I will feed my flock, and I will cause them to lie down. . . . I will seek that which was lost, and bring again that which was driven away . . . and I will set up one shepherd over them, and he shall feed them" (Ezek. 34:15-16, 23).

The star closest to Capella is an extraordinary star, called by astronomers Epsilon Aurigae. It is one of the largest of all stars that have been measured. We can get an idea of just how large this star is by comparing its size to that of our own solar system. The planet closest to the sun is Mercury; the second one is Venus. Our earth is the third planet at a distance of almost 93 million miles from the sun. Beyond Earth is Mars. Farther yet is the asteroid belt. Much farther is Jupiter and Saturn. Now, if the center of the star Epsilon Aurigae were placed where our sun is, the radius of that star would extend out beyond the orbit of Mercury, beyond Venus, beyond Earth, beyond Mars, beyond the asteroids, beyond Jupiter, and far beyond the orbit of Saturn. We on Earth would be orbiting in the middle of that star.

We can review many of these winter stars by locating the Heavenly **G**, a group of nine bright stars in the shape of a giant letter **G**. It is traced from Aldebaran in Taurus, to Capella in Auriga, over to Castor and Pollux in the constellation Gemini the Twins, down to Procyon in

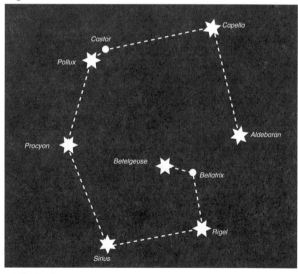

A "G" of stars

Canis Minor, over to Sirius in Canis Major, up to Rigel in Orion, then up to Bellatrix, and finally to Betelgeuse. Most of these stars are the very bright first-magnitude stars.

The brilliant stars overhead remind us of the psalmist's rejoicing that "the heavens declare the glory of God; and the firmament sheweth his handywork" (Ps. 19:1). The Bible portrays God not only as the Creator of these wonders in the sky but also as a loving Savior.

AND THE CHAMBERS OF THE SOUTH

JOB 9:9

Orion

Canis Major

Lepus

Eridanus

Fornax

Columba

Pyxis

Puppis

Horologium

Pictor

Dorado

Cetus

Vela

Carina

Reticulum

Volans

Phoenix

Crater

Hydra

Chamaeleon

Tucana

Musca

Octans

Hydrus

Crux

Apus

Corvus

Centaurus

Triangulum
Australe

Grus

Aquarius

Pava

Virgo

Circinus

Indus

Norma

Ara

Piscis Austrinus

Lupus

Telescopium

Libra

Corona Australis

Scorpius

Capricornus

Sagittarius

Serpens

Ophiuchus

Southern constellations

THE SOUTHERN STARS

To an observer on the earth the stars are continually changing in appearance. From our latitude the stars seem to rise in the
east at an angle every evening and set in the west at the same
angle. The reason the stars seem to rise and set is that the earth
is a spherical body rotating on its axis from west to east, and this
easterly rotation makes everything in the sky appear to move
from east to west.

But as we change latitude on the earth, the appearance of the
sky changes as well. As we travel toward the north, the stars rise
at an increasingly less steep angle, until at the North Pole the
stars do not rise at all but simply circle the North Star, which appears directly overhead. If we travel southward, the stars rise at
an ever increasing angle, until at the equator they rise straight up
in the east and set straight down in the west.

Over 2,000 years before Copernicus, Isaiah wrote, "Hast thou
not known? hast thou not heard, that the everlasting God, the
Lord, the Creator of the ends of the earth, fainteth not, neither is
weary? there is no searching of his understanding. . . . It is he
that sitteth upon the circle of the earth, and the inhabitants
thereof are as grasshoppers" (Isa. 40:28, 22).

It is a great comfort to the Christian to know that he serves
an omnipotent and omnipresent God. Whether he looks up at
the stars from remote tropical lands or from the frozen north-
land, he knows that God is there. The psalmist addresses the
Lord and says, "Whither shall I go from thy spirit? or whither
shall I flee from thy presence? If I ascend up into heaven, thou
art there: if I make my bed in hell, behold, thou art there. If I
take the wings of the morning, and dwell in the uttermost parts

of the sea; even there shall thy hand lead me, and thy right hand shall hold me. If I say, Surely the darkness shall cover me; even the night shall be light about me" (Ps. 139:7-11).

In addition to teaching that God is present everywhere, this passage contains the interesting fact that the night sky is not as dark as it looks. Even when there is no moon, there is light filtering down from the sky. The stars can account for only about 15 or 20 percent of this light. Some of it comes from the zodiacal light, which is light from our sun scattered by interstellar dust. But there are also other sources for it, such as the permanent general aurora.

From the equator every star in the sky rises and sets. There is no area that is always visible and none that is invisible. Here the constellation Virgo the Virgin, which we are used to seeing lower in the south, is high overhead. In the north the Big Dipper still points to the North Star, which is now obscured by the horizon. Toward the west Leo the Lion is farther to the north than we have seen it before.

But in the south is a whole group of stars that is quite new to us. Starting from Virgo the Virgin, we notice the little constellation Corvus the Crow. Alongside of Corvus is Crater the Cup. From Corvus we thread our way southward to the famous Southern Cross. Its shape is not as beautiful and symmetrical as the Northern Cross, but it is far more celebrated. The Southern Cross is featured in the flags of Australia and New Zealand and is on the coat of arms of Brazil, which is often called "the land of the Southern Cross."

The Southern Cross (the Crux) is easily confused with four other stars, often called "the false cross." This group is a little to the west of the Southern Cross and is formed by parts of the two constellations Carina and Vela. There are several ways of testing which group is the right one. The vertical staff of the Southern Cross points toward the South Pole, whereas that of the false cross does not. This feature corresponds to the pointers of the

Big Dipper in the northern hemisphere. But there are also pointers that point toward the Southern Cross. The two brightest stars in the area, Alpha and Beta Centauri, point to the top of the Southern Cross.

The constellation Centaurus is an interesting sight to viewers in the southern hemisphere. It practically surrounds the Southern Cross and covers a wide area. Its brightest star is Alpha Centauri, which is actually a group of three stars orbiting around one another. The smallest of them, Proxima Centauri, is famous as the closest star to our own sun.

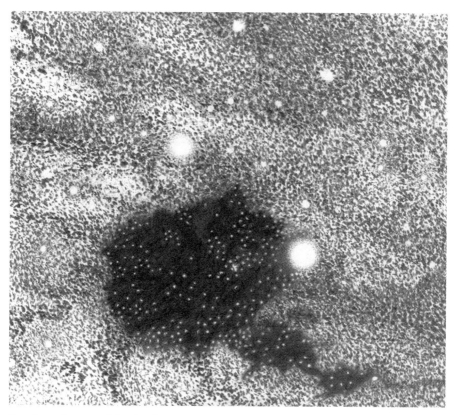

Southern Cross and Coalsack

Very close to the Southern Cross is the dark nebula called the "Coalsack." Early astronomers thought this dark region to be a hole in the stars that looked out upon empty space. With the aid of better telescopes and instruments, astronomers have discovered that the darkness is due to a cloud of dust and gas that obscures the light of the stars behind it. It is formed of dust like the bright clouds, but looks black because there are no stars close enough to illumine the dust particles. We really see it in silhouette against the light of the background stars.

Alongside of the Southern Cross and south of the Great Dog is the constellation that the ancients called Argo the Ship. Modern astronomers have divided Argo into three constellations after the parts of an ancient ship: Carina the Keel, Vela the Sail, and Puppis the Poop. The brightest star of Carina is Canopus, the southernmost first-magnitude star that can be seen from the southern United States. South of Orion and Lepus is the small constellation Columba the Dove. South of Sagittarius is Corona Australis, the Southern Crown; south of Scorpius is the constellation Ara the Altar. South of Pisces and Aries is the large constellation Cetus the Sea Monster.

While we watch the silent stars pass overhead, we cannot help thinking of the awesome majesty and grace of God: majesty in that He is able to create so vast a universe, and grace in that He takes notice of poor sinners like you and me. Among the constellations of the sky the Lord placed a cross in the northern hemisphere and a cross in the southern hemisphere as though to remind all mankind of the sacrifice of His Son for the sins of the world. If you do not know the Lord Jesus Christ as your personal Savior, we invite you to put your trust in Him. For Scripture says, "Believe on the Lord Jesus Christ, and thou shalt be saved" (Acts 16:31).

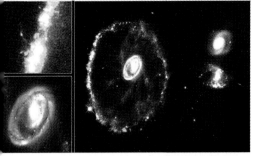

Cartwheel Galaxy

A rare and spectacular head-on collision between two galaxies appears in this NASA Hubble Space Telescope true-color image of the Cartwheel Galaxy, located 500 million light-years away in the constellation Sculptor.

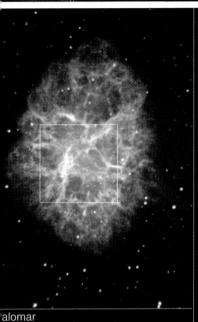

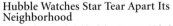

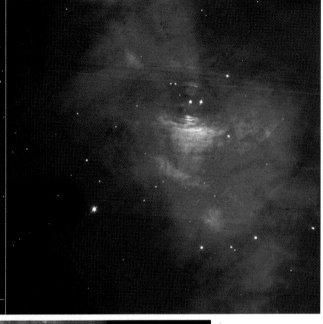

Crab Nebula

A new sequence of Hubble Space Telescope images of the remnant of a tremendous stellar explosion is giving astronomers a remarkable look at the dynamic relationship between the tiny Crab Pulsar and the vast nebula that it powers.

Hubble Watches Star Tear Apart Its Neighborhood

he shell of material, dubbed the Crescent Nebula NGC 6888), surrounds the "hefty," aging star WR 36, an extremely rare and short-lived class of a uper-hot star called a Wolf-Rayet. Hubble's multi-olored picture reveals with unprecedented clarity nat the shell of matter is a network of filaments nd dense knots.

An Expanding Bubble in Space

Astronomers, using the Wide Field Planetary Camera 2 on board NASA's Hubble Space Telescope in October and November 1997 and April 1999, imaged the Bubble Nebula (NGC 7635) with unprecedented clarity.

73

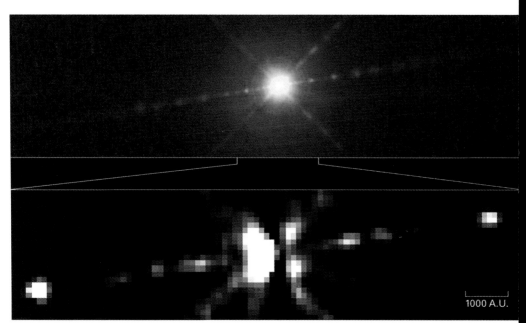

1000 A.U.

He2-90's Appearance Deceives Astronomers

Astronomers using NASA's Hubble Space Telescope have stumbled upon a mysterious object that is grudgingly yielding clues to its identity. A quick glance at the Hubble picture shows that this celestial body, called He2-90, looks like a young, dust-enshrouded star with narrow jets of material streaming from each side. But it's not. The object is classified as a planetary nebula, the glowing remains of a dying, lightweight star. But the Hubble observations suggest that it may not fit that classification either. The Hubble astronomers now suspect that this enigmatic object may actually be a pair of aging stars masquerading as a single youngster. One member of the duo is a bloated red giant star shedding matter from its outer layers. This matter is then gravitationally captured in a rotating, pancake-shaped accretion disk around a compact partner, which is most likely a young white dwarf (the collapsed remnant of a sun-like star). The stars cannot be seen in the Hubble images because a lane of dust obscures them.

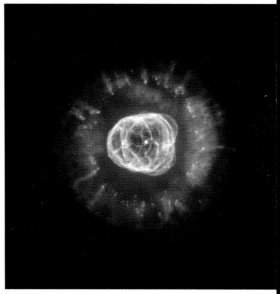

Hubble Reopens Eye on the Universe

This planetary nebula, the glowing remains of a dying, sun-like star, first spied by William Herschel in 1787, is nicknamed the "Eskimo" Nebula (NGC 2392) because, when viewed through ground-based telescopes, it resembles a face surrounded by a fur parka.

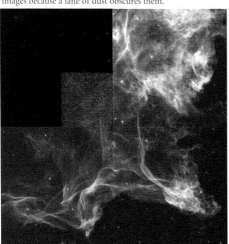

Hubble's Close-up View of a Shockwave from a Stellar Explosion

This image shows a small portion of a nebula called the "Cygnus Loop." Covering a region of the sky six times the diameter of the full moon, the Cygnus Loop is actually the expanding blastwave from a stellar cataclysm—a supernova explosion. In this image, the supernova blast wave, which is moving from left to right across the field of view, has recently hit a cloud of denser-than-average interstellar gas. This collision drives shock waves into the cloud that heat the interstellar gas, causing it to glow.

↟ Hubble Snaps Picture of Remarkable Double Cluster

These two dazzling clusters of stars, called NGC 1850, are found in one of our neighboring galaxies, the Large Magellanic Cloud. The photo's center is a young, globular-like star cluster. The smaller second cluster is below and to the right of the main cluster.

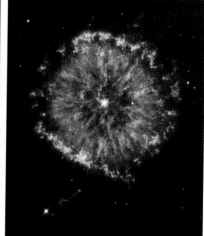

↟ "Ant Nebula"

The Hubble telescope has spied a giant celestial "eye," known as planetary nebula NGC 6751. Glowing in the constellation Aquila, the nebula is a cloud of gas ejected several thousand years ago from the hot star visible in its center.

Hourglass Nebula

...is is an image of MyCn18, a young planetary nebula located about 8,000 light-...ars away, taken with the Wide Field and Planetary Camera 2 (WFPC2) aboard ...SA's Hubble Space Telescope (HST). This Hubble image reveals the true shape of ...yCn18 to be an hourglass with an intricate pattern of "etchings" in its walls.

Butterfly Nebula

M2-9, also known as Twin Jet Nebula, is a striking example of a "butterfly," or bipolar, planetary nebula.

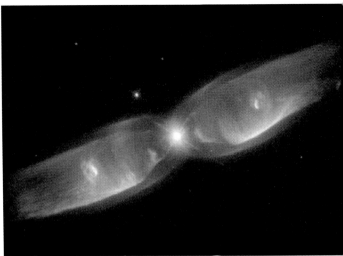

NGC 3603

This giant galactic nebula, formed by a supergiant star called Sher 25, has a unique circumstellar ring of glowing gas. Near the center of the view is a so-called starburst cluster.

⬆ Egg Nebula

This image of the Egg Nebula, also known as CRL2688 and located roughly 3,000 light-years from us, was taken in red light. The nebula is really a large cloud of dust and gas ejected by the star, expanding at a speed of 20 km/s (115,000 mph). A dense cocoon of dust (the dark band in the image's center) enshrouds the star and hides it from our view.

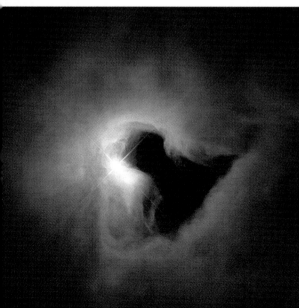

⬅ Hubble Takes a Close-up View of a Reflection Nebula in Orion

Just weeks after NASA astronauts repaired the Hubble Space Telescope in December 1999, the Hubble Heritage Project snapped this picture of NGC 1999, a nebula in the constellation Orion. The Heritage astronomers, in collaboration with scientists in Texas and Ireland, used Hubble's Wide Field Planetary Camera 2 (WFPC2) to obtain the color image.

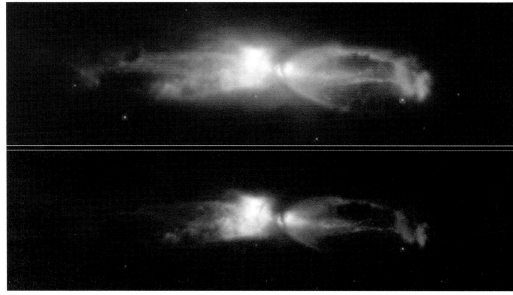

⬆ The "Rotten Egg" Nebula: A Planetary Nebula in the Making

This star, with the prosaic name of OH231.8+4.2, is seen in these infrared pictures to be blowing out gas and dust in two opposite directions. So much dust has been cast off and now surrounds the star that it cannot be seen directly; only its starlight that is reflected off the dust can be seen.

Solar Prominence ⬌

This Extreme Ultraviolet Imaging Telescope (EIT) image of a huge, handle-shaped prominence was taken on September 14, 1999, in the 304 angstrom wavelength. Prominences are huge clouds of relatively cool, dense plasma suspended in the sun's hot, thin corona.

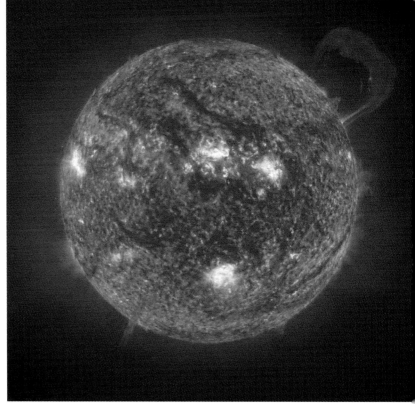

78

Cosmic Magnifying Glass

Scanning the heavens for the first time since the successful December 1999 servicing mission, NASA's Hubble Space Telescope has imaged a giant, cosmic magnifying glass, a massive cluster of galaxies called Abell 218. This hefty cluster resides in the constellation Draco, some 2 billion light-years from Earth.

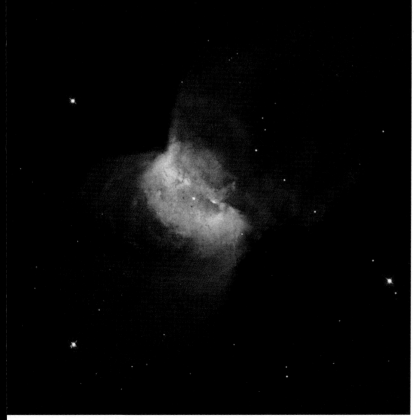

⬅ NGC 2346
Planetary Nebula

NGC 2346 is remarkable because its central star is known to be actually a very close pair of stars, orbiting each other every 16 days. NGC 2346 lies about 2,000 light-years away from us and is about one-third of a light-year in size.

Massive Star Cluster ⟹
NASA's Hubble Space Telescope has taken a "family portrait" of young, ultra-bright stars nested in their embryonic cloud of glowing gases.

⬇ Ghostly Reflections in the Pleiades
This ghostly apparition is actually an interstellar cloud caught in the process of destruction by strong radiation from a nearby hot star. This picture shows a cloud illuminated by light from the bright star Merope. Located in the Pleiades star cluster, the cloud is called IC 349 or Barnard's Merope Nebula.

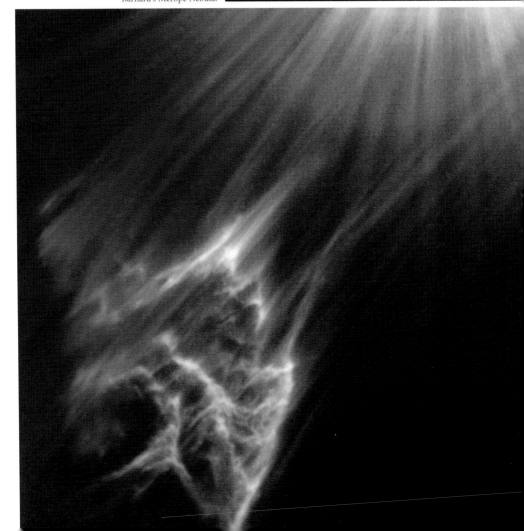

Mars Surface with Big Joe Rock

Near the Viking 1 Lander on the Chryse Plains of Mars, "Big Joe" keeps a silent vigil. This large, often-photographed dark rock has a topping of reddish fine-grained silt that spills down its sides. It is about 2 meters (6.6 feet) long and lies about 8 meters (26 feet) from the spacecraft.

Source of Ultraviolet Light

NASA Hubble Space Telescope's exquisite resolution has allowed astronomers to resolve, for the first time, images of hot blue stars deep inside an elliptical galaxy. Hubble confirms that the ultraviolet light comes from a population of extremely hot helium-burning stars at a late stage in their lives. The swarm of nearly 8,000 blue stars resembles a blizzard of snowflakes near the core of the neighboring galaxy M32, located 2.5 million light-years away in the constellation Andromeda.

Thackeray's Globules in IC 2944

In 1950, astronomer A. D. Thackeray first spied the globules' opaque dust clouds in IC 2944. IC 2944 is filled with gas and dust that is illuminated and heated by a loose cluster of massive stars. These stars are much hotter and much more massive than our sun.

Horsehead Nebula

The Horsehead is a cold, dark cloud of gas and dust silhouetted against the bright nebula IC 434.

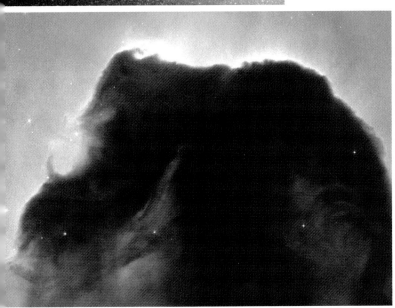

⬆ Eagle Nebula

These eerie, dark, pillar-like structures are actually columns of cool
interstellar hydrogen gas and dust
that protrude from the interior
wall of a dark molecular cloud like
stalagmites from the floor of a
cavern. They are part of the "Eagle
nebula" (also called M16—the
16th object in Charles Messier's
18th-century catalog of "fuzzy"
objects that aren't comets).

Satellite Footprints ⬌
Seen in Jupiter Aurora

A curtain of glowing gas is
wrapped around Jupiter's north
pole like a lasso. This curtain of
light, called an aurora, is produced
when high-energy electrons race
along the planet's magnetic field
and into the upper atmosphere
where they excite atmospheric
gases, causing them to glow.

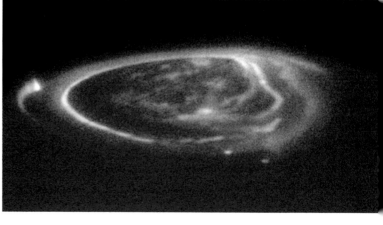

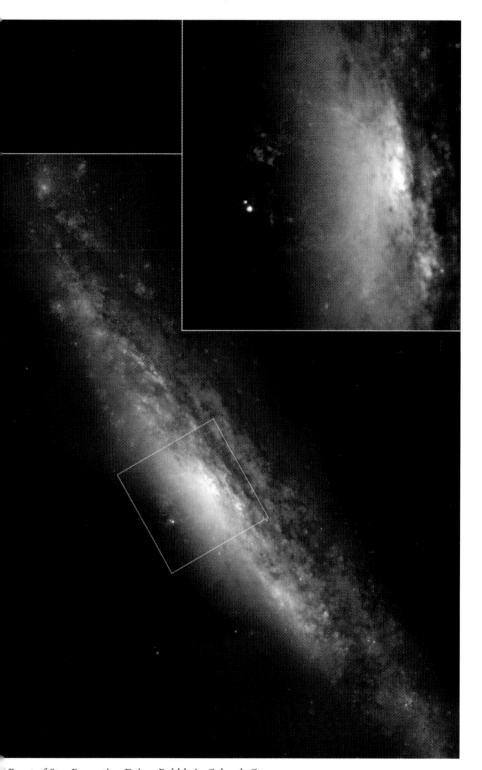

Burst of Star Formation Drives Bubble in Galaxy's Core

hese snapshots reveal dramatic activities within the core of the galaxy NGC 3079, where a lumpy bubble of hot
s is rising from a cauldron of glowing matter. The picture at left shows the bubble in the center of the galaxy's
sk. The structure is more than 3,000 light-years wide and rises 3,500 light-years above the galaxy's disk. The
naller photo at right is a close-up view of the bubble.

Neptune

This picture of Neptune was produced from the last whole planet images taken through the green and orange filters on the Voyager 2 narrow angle camera. The images were taken at a range of 4.4 million miles from the planet, 4 days and 20 hours before closest approach. The picture shows the Great Dark Spot and its companion bright smudge.

Mercury

The Image Processing Lab at NASA's Jet Propulsion Laboratory produced this photomosaic of Mercury's southern hemisphere using computer software and techniques developed for use in processing planetary data. The Mariner 10 spacecraft imaged the region during its initial flyby of the planet.

Pluto

This is the clearest view yet of the distant planet Pluto and its moon, Charon, as revealed by NASA's Hubble Space Telescope (HST). The image was taken by the European Space Agency's Faint Object Camera on February 21, 1994, when the planet was 2.6 billion miles (4.4 billion kilometers) from Earth, or nearly 30 times the separation between Earth and the sun. Hubble's corrected optics show the two objects as clearly separate and sharp disks. This now allows astronomers to measure directly (to within about 1 percent) Pluto's diameter of 1440 miles (2320 kilometers) and Charon's diameter of 790 miles (1270 kilometers).

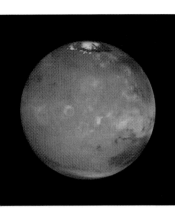

Mars

The telescope's Wide Field and Planetary Camera 2 snapped these images between April 27 and May 6, when Mars was 54 million miles (87 million kilometers) from Earth. From this distance the telescope could see Martian features as small as 12 miles (19 kilometers) wide. This image is centered on the region of the planet known as Tharsis, home of the largest volcanoes in the solar system. The bright, ring-like feature just to the left of center is the volcano Olympus Mons, which is more than 340 miles (550 kilometers) across and 17 miles (27 kilometers) high.

"Backwards" Spiral Galaxy

To the surprise of astronomers, the galaxy NGC 4622 appears to be rotating in the opposite direction from what they expected.

Saturn & Moons

This montage of images of the Saturnian system was prepared from an assemblage of images taken by the Voyager 1 spacecraft during its Saturn encounter in November 1980. This artist's view shows Dione in the forefront, Saturn rising behind, Tethys and Mimas fading in the distance to the right, Enceladus and Rhea off Saturn's rings to the left, and Titan in its distant orbit at the top.

Saturn B-Ring Closeup

This view shows some detail and differences in the complex system of rings. The "reddening" of the B-ring on the unlit side was also seen in Voyager 1 images. Voyager 2 obtained this picture from a range of 3.4 million kilometers (2.1 million miles) through the clear, green, and violet filters.

⬆ Saturn

Because Saturn's north pole is currently tilted toward Earth (24 degrees), the HST image reveals unprecedented detail in atmospheric features at the northern polar hood, a region not extensively imaged by the Voyager space probes. The classic features of Saturn's vast ring system are also clearly seen from outer to inner edge: the bright A and B rings, divided by the Cassini division, and the very faint inner C ring. The Enche division, a dark gap near the outer edge of the A ring, has never before been photographed from Earth.

⬅ Saturn's C-Ring Closeup

This Voyager 2 view, focusing on Saturn's C-ring (and to a lesser extent, the B-ring at top and left) was compiled from three separate images taken through ultraviolet, clear, and green filters.

⬇ Jupiter & Moons

Jupiter and its four planet-size moons, called the Galilean satellites, were photographed in early March 1979 by Voyager 1 and assembled into this collage. Reddish Io (upper left) is nearest Jupiter, then Europa (center), Ganymede, and Callisto (lower right).

⬆ Venus

This ultraviolet-light image of the planet Venus was taken on January 24, 1995, when Venus was at a distance of 70.6 million miles (113.6 million kilometers) from Earth. Venus is covered with clouds made of sulfuric acid, rather than the water-vapor clouds found on Earth.

⬆ Uranus

This computer enhancement of a Voyager 2 image emphasizes the high-level haze in Uranus' upper atmosphere. Clouds are obscured by the overlying atmosphere.

⬇ Jupiter's Moons

This image, taken by NASA's Galileo spacecraft, shows a new blue-colored volcanic plume extending about 100 kilometers (about 60 miles) into space from Jupiter's moon Io (see inset at lower left). The blue color of the plume is consistent with the presence of sulfur dioxide gas and "snow" condensing from the gas as the plume expands and cools. The images at right show a comparison of changes seen near the volcano Ra Patera since the Voyager spacecraft flybys of 1979 (windows at right show Voyager image at top and Galileo image at bottom).

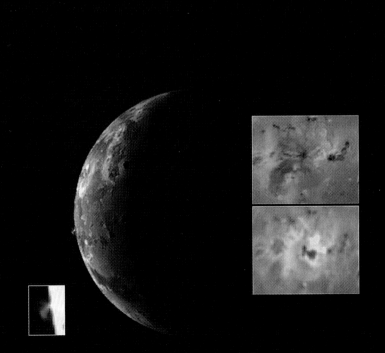

AND, LO, THE STAR, WHICH THEY SAW IN THE EAST,
WENT BEFORE THEM

MATTHEW 2:9

THE STAR OF WONDER

"And it came to pass in those days, that there went out a decree from Caesar Augustus, that all the world should be taxed. (And this taxing was first made when Cyrenius was governor of Syria.) And all went to be taxed, every one into his own city. And Joseph also went up from Galilee, out of the city of Nazareth, into Judaea, unto the city of David, which is called Bethlehem; (because he was of the house and lineage of David:) to be taxed with Mary his espoused wife, being great with child. And so it was, that, while they were there, the days were accomplished that she should be delivered. And she brought forth her firstborn son, and wrapped him in swaddling clothes, and laid him in a manger; because there was no room for them in the inn. And there were in the same country shepherds abiding in the field, keeping watch over their flock by night. And, lo, the angel of the Lord came upon them, and the glory of the Lord shone round about them: and they were sore afraid. And the angel said unto them, Fear not: for, behold, I bring you good tidings of great joy, which shall be to all people. For unto you is born this day in the city of David a Saviour, which is Christ the Lord. And this shall be a sign unto you; Ye shall find the babe wrapped in swaddling clothes, lying in a manger. And suddenly there was with the angel a multitude of the heavenly host praising God, and saying, Glory to God in the highest, and on earth peace, good will toward men. And it came to pass, as the angels were gone away from them into heaven, the shepherds said one to another, Let us now go even unto Bethlehem, and see this thing which is come to pass, which the Lord hath made known unto us. And they came with haste, and found Mary, and Joseph, and the babe lying in a manger" (Luke 2:1-16).

"Now when Jesus was born in Bethlehem of Judaea in the days of Herod the king, behold, there came wise men from the east to Jerusalem, Saying, Where is he that is born King of the Jews? for we have seen his star in the east, and are come to worship him. When Herod the king had heard these things, he was troubled, and all

Jerusalem with him. And when he had gathered all the chief priests and scribes of the people together, he demanded of them where Christ should be born. And they said unto him, In Bethlehem of Judaea: for thus it is written by the prophet, And thou Bethlehem, in the land of Juda, art not the least among the princes of Juda: for out of thee shall come a Governor, that shall rule my people Israel. Then Herod, when he had privily called the wise men, inquired of them diligently what time the star appeared. And he sent them to Bethlehem, and said, Go and search diligently for the young child; and when ye have found him, bring me word again, that I may come and worship him also. When they had heard the king, they departed; and, lo, the star, which they saw in the east, went before them, till it came and stood over where the young child was. When they saw the star, they rejoiced with exceeding great joy. And when they were come into the house, they saw the young child with Mary his mother, and fell down, and worshipped him: and when they had opened their treasures, they presented unto him gifts; gold, and frankincense, and myrrh. And being warned of God in a dream that they should not return to Herod, they departed into their own country another way" (Matt. 2:1-12).

At the Christmas season the question naturally arises, what was the "star of wonder" the wise men saw in the east? In order to answer this question we will need to reconstruct the skies as they appeared at the time of the Savior's birth. First, however, we must determine when the Lord was born. It is not so simple a matter as counting back the number of years in our calendar to the year one. As peculiar as it may sound, Christ was actually born several years before Christ. This apparent paradox is easily explained because the present calendar was not established until A.D. 533. Before that time the Roman system of figuring from the founding of the city of Rome was used. In the year A.D. 533 a Roman monk, Dionysius Exiguus, introduced a new calendar figuring from the birth of Christ. Dionysius had found a statement in the writings of Clement of Alexandria that Christ was born in the twenty-eighth year of the reign of Augustus Caesar. Dionysius accepted it as accurate and based his calculations on it; what he did not know is that for four years before the beginning of the reign of the emperor Augustus he had been reigning under his own name, Octavius. After he had reigned for four years, the Roman Senate awarded him the title Augustus.

With this beginning we must piece together clues from astronomy and history. It is surprising how many inaccuracies are in popular belief. Christmas cards portray the wise men and the shepherds coming together to visit the newborn King, yet the Scriptures record them as coming separately. They show shepherds looking up at the star of Bethlehem although the shepherds never saw the star.

What facts can be determined? Scripture tells us that Jesus was born in the days of Herod the king. The Jewish historian

The Holy Family with Young John the Baptist *by Giuseppe Bottani, Roman, 1717-1787. From the Bob Jones University collection.*

Josephus tells us that Herod died a few days after an eclipse of the moon that could be seen from Jericho and that after a week of mourning for Herod the feast of the passover was celebrated. Now the passover and eclipses are events which astronomers can calculate from the motion of the moon in its orbit. The only eclipse which was visible in that part of the world shortly before a passover took place was on March 13, 4 B.C. The passover was observed on April 12 of that year. This means that Jesus was born before 4 B.C. But how long before?

Another clue is the decree of taxation made by Caesar Augustus. A few years ago archaeologists working in Ankara, Turkey, found a list of the years that decrees for tax collection were issued. The only date which comes close to the time under discussion was the year 8 B.C. It may very well be, however, that the actual collection of taxes took place a year or two later in the outer provinces of the empire, such as Palestine.

Now we have found the outside limits for the time of our Savior's birth. It was after 8 B.C. but before 4 B.C. Of the three intervening years let us pick the median year, 6 B.C., as the approximate time of the birth of the Lord.

There is one further clue to the time of year that all this took place. Luke tells us that there were "shepherds abiding in the field, keeping watch over their flock by night" (Luke 2:8). Shepherds do not normally watch their flocks at night except in the spring when the lambs are being born. Thus, it seems probable that the Lord was born sometime in the spring of 6 B.C. We have no more clues that would narrow it down any further.

What was in the skies back in the spring of 6 B.C. that would have attracted the attention of the wise men? Many suggestions have been made. The Greek word for star, *aster,* may refer to a star, a meteor, a comet, or a planet. In ancient literature it is used for all of these.

Some have thought that the star was nothing more than a bright meteor, or fireball. However, such large meteors are

Comet Morehouse

burned up in a few seconds by the friction of the earth's atmosphere, and anyone who watches the sky consistently, as the wise men no doubt did, can expect to see several of them in a lifetime. They would not have regarded such a meteor as particularly significant. Furthermore, such a brief flash of light does not coincide with the description that Scripture gives of the star.

Other men have thought that the star was a comet. A bright comet can be a very impressive sight; however, in ancient times the appearance of a comet was almost universally held to be a portent of disaster—an evil omen of war, pestilence, or famine—and not a good sign. Therefore, the comet theory must also be rejected.

Still others have thought that the star was a nova. Every so often a bright nova, or "new star," appears in the sky. It is not really a new star. It has been there all along, but it has been so dim and insignificant that no one has noticed it. Then suddenly the star seems to explode, and in a few days it may increase in brightness thousands of times. An ordinary nova may give off 25,000 times as much light as our sun, but a great supernova may become 100 million times brighter than our sun. Such a supernova can be seen in broad daylight and is brighter than anything in the night sky except the moon. After a few months a nova will dim to its former obscurity, and sometimes hardly more than a cloud of luminous gas seems to remain around the much weakened star.

Such a nova does not seem to fit the circumstances of the Biblical account. There is no record of the appearance of a nova at anytime near the Lord's birth. It is always possible to say that a nova appeared, without any record of it. However, an argument from silence is always uncertain. It is better to investigate another possibility.

We must remember one thing. When the wise men came to Jerusalem and mentioned the star, no one knew about it. Herod especially would not be slow to recognize a sign in the sky that portended a change of his rulership! But Herod knew nothing about it, for he enquired "diligently what time the star appeared" (Matt. 2:7). Now this means one of two things: either the sky looked much as it always does and held special significance only to the wise men, or else only the wise men could see the star. Let us examine the first of these possibilities.

If what appeared in the sky to the wise men was plainly visible to all, we must determine what was in the sky in the spring of 6 B.C. The great astronomer Kepler made some discoveries in A.D. 1604 that will help us to answer this question. In that year Kepler observed a close grouping of the planets Jupiter, Saturn, and Mars. He began to calculate the orbits of these planets in order to see when this combination had occurred before, and he discovered that this grouping of the planets could happen only once in 805 years. Counting back 2 such periods, we find that it did occur in the spring of 6 B.C.

Jupiter takes almost 12 years to complete its orbit around the sun, and Saturn takes almost 30 years to do the same. In 7 B.C. Jupiter slowly overtook Saturn and passed it. When a planet passes another, astronomers say that they are in conjunction. After that conjunction the earth in its orbit overtook Jupiter, making it appear to move backward in the sky, and for the second time in 7 B.C. Jupiter and Saturn were in conjunction, this time as Jupiter moved back past Saturn in the opposite direction. But then Jupiter's forward motion asserted itself, and

Jupiter passed Saturn for the third time in a few months, producing a triple conjunction which can occur only once in 125 years!

This phenomenon must have impressed the wise men greatly. But while Jupiter and Saturn were still close together, the planet Mars, moving much faster in its orbit than either of the others, passed both of them. This grouping can occur only once in 805 years, and it must have astounded the wise men. All these events took place in the constellation Pisces the Fish, which the ancient astrologers called the "House of the Hebrews," because planets in that area were supposed to refer to the Jews.

Astrology is just a system of fortune telling. Neither the Bible nor science would approve of it. But these wise men were not fortune-tellers. They were from the East—no doubt, from Persia—where there were many Jews living. They had surely heard of Balaam's prophecy in the Old Testament that "There shall come a Star out of Jacob, and a Sceptre shall rise out of Israel" (Num. 24:17). They may very well have had God's revelation that this prophecy was to be fulfilled.

The planets in their conjunctions may have been an indication to the wise men. Unquestionably, these phenomena were visible in the sky at the time. But since they do not completely fit with the Scriptural account, we are left with the other possibility that only the wise men could see the star.

They claimed that they had seen the star in the east, although these planets are setting in the west. It is true that that verse may be interpreted to mean that they saw the star when they were in the East, but apparently they had not seen the star since, because after they had left Herod, they were astonished to see the star again. And Scripture says, "When they saw the star, they rejoiced with exceeding great joy" (Matt. 2:10). This account, taken at face value, implies that they had not seen the star since they had left the East. The planets, however, would have been visible every night.

The Scriptural account also says that "the star, which they saw in the east, went before them" (Matt. 2:9). In the original Greek the verb used in this sentence is an imperfect tense, which indicates continued action. Literally it reads, "The star was going before them, until it came and stood over where the little child was." No natural star could do what this verse describes. A star overhead at Bethlehem would also be overhead at Jerusalem. This star moved among the stars and guided the wise men.

If all men could have seen the star, there would have been an army of Herod's troops following the star in order to slay the newborn King. But no, only the wise men could see the star. Even today it is only men of spiritual understanding who can see the "star of wonder" and can enter into the true meaning of Christmas.

This explanation is not needlessly multiplying the supernatural. The virgin birth of the Lord was a miracle of momentous importance. When the divine Son of God became incarnate in human flesh, God performed the greatest miracle that mankind has seen. The wise men came as representatives of the Gentiles to give homage to Him who is to rule all nations. It is entirely appropriate that a miracle should guide them to the right person and place.

The early Christian martyr Ignatius wrote to the Ephesians about the birth of the Lord and said, "How then was he manifested to the world? A star shone in heaven beyond all the stars, and its light was inexpressible, and its newness caused astonishment." He is speaking of the spiritual effect of the glorious gospel of Christ as a light shining in a dark place. The Lord Jesus Christ did not come to earth to live, but to die for the sins of the world. As the angel said to Joseph, "Thou shalt call his name JESUS: for he shall save his people from their sins" (Matt. 1:21).

THE SUN TO RULE BY DAY: FOR HIS MERCY
ENDURETH FOR EVER

PSALM 136:8

THE PORTRAIT OF A STAR:
OUR SUN

Our familiar sun is a star. It is a very average star—average in size and average in temperature. Among the stars some are much cooler than our sun and others much hotter. Some stars are no bigger than our planet, whereas others are much larger than the orbit of our earth around the sun. The other stars are so far away from us that most are just pinpoints of light in even the greatest telescopes. Because our sun is so close to us, it is the most convenient of the stars to study.

Astronomers estimate that the sun has a diameter of slightly more than 864,000 miles. It would take about 332,000 times the mass of the earth to equal the mass of the sun. This huge mass of the sun is the center of the solar system, and all the planets revolve around it at their respective distances. The orbit of the earth is approximately 93 million miles from the sun.

When the sun rises, we can immediately perceive the heat and light that emanate from it. But what we perceive is only a small fraction of the energy it is putting forth, most of which is being lost in outer space as it radiates in other directions.

The sun is a sphere of gas that is very dense toward the center but thins out toward the surface. The center of the sun is actually a great nuclear reactor that operates at temperatures of many millions of degrees. This nuclear energy is radiated out from the surface of the sun in an unbelievable volume. Scientists estimate that the sun is radiating 70,000 horsepower per square yard of its surface. In brilliance each square inch of the sun is shining with 1,500,000 candlepower. When you consider how many square inches there are on the sun, it is no wonder that it is a blindingly brilliant object in the skies.

Men have always regarded the sun as the source of great blessings, and rightly so. Our sun supplies the earth with all the heat and energy it needs in order to sustain life. If the sun were to disappear, the earth would soon become a solid mass of ice. The oceans would freeze all the way to the bottom; even the atmosphere would freeze. The psalmist tells us that God designed the sun for the good of the earth. He has "set a tabernacle for the sun, which is as a bridegroom coming out of his chamber, and rejoiceth as a strong man to run a race. His going forth is from the end of the heaven, and his circuit unto the ends of it: and there is nothing hid from the heat thereof" (Ps. 19:4-6).

The apparent motion of the sun from east to west has been observed by all peoples, ancient and modern. The earth's rotation on its axis from west to east causes everything in the skies, including the sun, to appear to move from east to west. It is not so well known that the sun also rotates on its axis. A rotation of the sun requires about 25 days.

The most famous and striking events connected with the sun are the eclipses. An eclipse of the sun is produced when the moon passes between the earth and the sun. This action blots out the light of the sun in a narrow path that sweeps across the earth. In ancient times an eclipse was regarded as a portent of disaster or a foreshadowing of the fall of a king. The poet Milton expressed it well: "The sun . . . / In dim Eclipse, disastrous twilight sheds / On half the Nations, and with fear of change / Perplexes Monarchs."

Unquestionably, it is an impressive sight to see the brilliant sun grow dark as a strange shadow blots out its light. The atmosphere on earth becomes cooler; animals and birds act as if night were coming; the sky becomes dark. Just before the eclipse becomes total, a series of bright points of light twinkle as the sun glints past the craters of the moon. These twinkling lights are called Baily's Beads, after the astronomer who first described them. Then, suddenly, it is a total eclipse. The stars shine. From the sun the beautiful corona extends its faint but glowing light, providing about as much light as the full moon. When an eclipse coincides with a sunspot maximum, the corona extends almost equally on all sides of the sun. When it is at the time of a sunspot minimum, the corona extends much farther along the equator than it does at the poles. An eclipse is one of the most beautiful sights in the heavens, but unfortunately a very brief one. In the next instant the sun peeks out from behind the moon. The eclipse is over; the corona disappears; the stars fade away. When a photographer can capture the instant that the sun appears, the pictures show a famous diamond-ring appearance. This also is a very short-lived phenomenon, because the shadow rapidly disappears and the sun regains its brilliance.

The Scriptures warn us that the sun will be darkened in the day that the Lord pours out His wrath upon the sinfulness of mankind. The prophet Joel describes that time of punishment and wrath by saying, "The sun shall be turned into darkness, and the moon into blood, before the great and the terrible day of the Lord come" (Joel 2:31).

The sun is a prominent topic in the Scriptures. It is mentioned at least 154 times. From the beginning it appears as an object created by God: "And God made two great lights; the greater light to rule the day, and the lesser light to rule the night: he made the stars also. And God set them in the firmament of the heaven to give light upon the earth" (Gen. 1:16-17). It was designed by God expressly to meet the need of man. The psalmist recognized this merciful provision for man and gives praise "To him that made great lights: for his mercy endureth for ever: The sun to rule by day: for his mercy endureth for ever" (Ps. 136:7-8). This great natural blessing God graciously gives to all men, "for he maketh his sun to rise on the evil and on the good, and sendeth rain on the just and on the unjust" (Matt. 5:45). In the same gracious manner God has provided a way of salvation through the person of His Son, the Lord Jesus Christ.

The sun is the object of several outstanding miracles in Scripture. When Joshua led the Israelites against the kings of the Amorites, he saw he could not defeat the whole coalition in one day. So he did a remarkable thing. "Then spake Joshua to the Lord in the day when the Lord delivered up the Amorites before the children of Israel, and he said in the sight of Israel, Sun, stand thou still upon Gibeon; and thou, Moon, in the valley of Ajalon. And the sun stood still, and the moon stayed, until the people had avenged themselves upon their enemies" (Josh. 10:12-13). The phrase means literally "the sun hasted not to go down." Expositors have speculated on how the Lord performed this miracle. Did the sun stop in its course? Did the rotation of the earth cease? Or, as is more in keeping with the phrase "hasted not," did the rotation of the earth slow down? Can this be explained as a refraction of light in which the relative motions of the heavenly bodies did not change? It is dangerous for the expositor to try to decide how God accomplished a supernatural miracle. The God who ordained natural law can certainly transcend natural law; how He does so is none of man's business. It is enough to say that Joshua's "long day" cannot be explained as a natural phenomenon but must be interpreted as a supernatural miracle. The Scripture adds, "And there was no day like that before it or after it, that the Lord hearkened unto the voice of a man: for the Lord fought for Israel" (Josh. 10:14). The Lord, by a unique miracle, enabled Joshua to defeat a coalition of enemies most thoroughly.

A miracle of similarly striking effect occurred when King Hezekiah prayed that the Lord spare his life. The Lord sent the prophet Isaiah to the king with the message that He had added 15 years to the king's life and offered the king a sign that the prophecy would be fulfilled: "And this shall be a sign unto thee from the Lord, that the Lord will do this thing that he hath spoken; behold, I will bring again the shadow of the degrees, which is gone down in the sun dial of Ahaz, ten degrees backward. So the sun returned ten degrees, by which degrees it was gone down" (Isa. 38:7-8). The dial was no doubt a large obelisk with a series of steps on each side, so that the obelisk acted as the gnomon of a regular sundial. This occurrence is another supernatural miracle and should not be interpreted merely as the sunlight glancing off a cloud. How God performs His miracles must be ascribed to His omnipotent power.

The last book of the Bible, Revelation, has a number of references to the sun. The Apostle John saw the vision of the Lord Jesus in His glory and said, "His countenance was as the sun shineth in his strength" (Rev. 1:16). The last mention of the sun in Scripture refers to the heavenly city, New Jerusalem: "The city had no need of the sun, neither of the moon, to shine in it: for the glory of God did lighten it, and the Lamb is the light thereof" (Rev. 21:23). It does not say that the sun and moon cease to exist, but just that they will not be needed in the glory of that day. Does God ever give us anything that is not needed? Of course He does. The sun will likely have a place in the new creation. Even if it may not, the glories of the future universe should not keep us from appreciating the splendors of the present one.

Astronomers are continually observing and classifying the surface phenomena of the sun. Visible on the sun from time to time are the strange phenomena called sunspots. Some of these are large enough to be seen without a telescope. Sunspots are not really black; they just appear that way when seen against the intensely bright surface of the sun, which is called the photosphere. Sunspots move with the rotation of the sun. The larger spots can last several rotations.

Although sunspots have been known for thousands of years and have been observed carefully for centuries, many things about them still puzzle astronomers. They know, for instance, that sunspots occur in cycles with a maximum approximately every eleven years. They also know that sunspots are connected with tremendous magnetic fields and that they usually travel in pairs. In one cycle the first spot will have a North Pole magnetic field and the following spot a South Pole magnetism. But in the next eleven-year cycle the polarity is reversed with the first spot a South Pole and the following one a North Pole. The solution of this mystery seems locked deep in the interior of the sun.

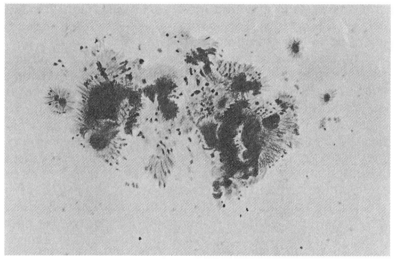

Sunspots

Most people know that a sunspot maximum produces severe electromagnetic disturbances in radio communications on earth,[1] and astronomers have put forth many theories to account for the far-reaching magnetic characteristics of sunspots. But it remains an open question actively debated by astronomers.

Above the surface of the sun, or photosphere, is a less dense layer called the chromosphere, which corresponds to our atmosphere. For a long time astronomers could view the chromosphere only during a total eclipse when the light from the photosphere is blotted out and the chromosphere appears as a bright ring around the sun's edge. But now astronomers have perfected instruments that enable them to observe the chromosphere without waiting for an eclipse.

[1] It may, however, enhance ten-meter propagation.

Solar corona

Above the chromosphere is a still rarer envelope of gases called the corona. This corona may be spread out for millions of miles around the sun. The temperature of the chromosphere and the corona has been one of the most perplexing phenomena for astronomers to explain. The temperature of the surface of the sun is estimated by astronomers to be 10,000° Fahrenheit (in terms of absolute degrees, about 6,000 kelvins). But the temperature in the middle of the chromosphere registers 50,000 kelvins. The thin corona has an estimated temperature of a million kelvins. Astronomers cannot explain these great jumps in temperature on the basis of radiation, for radiation diminishes in temperature as it travels from its source. The best explanation astronomers have thought of is that shock waves or sound waves coming from the surface of the sun build up energy in the chromosphere and the corona and produce such high temperatures. Intensive investigation is going on in order to account for this phenomenon.

Solar prominences

The phenomena known as solar prominences are particularly interesting to study. The type known as eruptive starts out by exploding from the surface of the sun, sometimes with a velocity of hundreds of miles a second. The eruptive prominence is really made up of a thin jet of incandescent gases that changes in its formation.

It is impressive to watch a prominence grow larger and larger as it expands upward from the sun's surface. The gases in a prominence are much more rarified than the atmosphere on earth, but they are so hot that they glow like the gas in a fluorescent lamp. It is not uncommon to find prominences that dwarf the size of the earth. Some prominences on record have leaped far beyond 100,000 miles upward from the surface of the sun. Other prominences seem to condense and fall like rain into the sun. Apparently they can draw upon the material in the sun's corona to maintain their distinctive forms.

When astronomers view a prominence from the top, they see a thin line, which they call a filament. It is only when filaments reach the edge of the sun that their shape appears in silhouette against the sky. They are often connected with sunspots, and certainly the magnetic fields in the sun play a big part in the growth and formation of solar prominences. Many times when a prominence has spent itself, another one will form in the same place and with the same shape. Astronomers draw volumes of information about the sun's magnetic fields by continually observing their form and motion.

It is only recently that astronomers have tried to record most of the solar flares. These are brief flashes of light in the sun's atmosphere that seem much like flashes of lightning on the earth. Solar flares discharge tremendous quantities of X-rays and ultraviolet radiation that can just about blot out radio communication on earth.

The sun's radiation on the earth's atmosphere is the cause of many phenomena on the earth, including the beautiful aurora borealis, the Northern Lights. In the higher latitudes it is a frequent sight. The auroras may take a great variety of different shapes and colors. However, our atmosphere, which manifests the beautiful auroras, is the cause of innumerable headaches for astronomers. All the telescopic observations of the sun and the stars suffer from the obscuring and distorting effects of our atmosphere. As far as astronomers are concerned, sighting objects through our atmosphere is like peering through a fog. This is why astronomers follow our space program so eagerly. They long for the day when observatories can be established on the moon or on another planet where an atmosphere does not exist. From such a vantage point, the sun with its magnificent corona extending out into space would not be obscured at all. Where there is no atmosphere, the stars shining in a black sky can be seen at the same time that the sun is in view.

Astronomers may regret the obscuring effect of the atmosphere, but they certainly appreciate its benefits. Without the great filtering action of the atmosphere, life on earth would be completely destroyed by the intense X-ray and ultraviolet radiation that the sun pours forth. The thick blanket of atmosphere makes life on earth possible.

Clearly God has designed man for a specific environment and has fitted his environment to him. Man leaves the protection of his earth home at his own risk. Many question the wisdom of man's attempts at space travel because heaven is God's domain. That is true, but the earth also belongs to God. As Scripture says, "The earth is the Lord's, and the fulness thereof; the world, and they that dwell therein" (Ps. 24:1). Sinful man is a trespasser upon the earth as well as in the heavens. Only a person who is right with God through accepting the work of the Lord Jesus Christ can expect peace and salvation in this world or out of it.

When we look up at the countless stars, we wonder, is the sun the only star that has life connected with it? Astronomy has no answer to that, but the Bible teaches that there are hundreds of millions of spiritual intelligences that do not have their home on the earth. Man himself must leave this earth at the time of his death, but his life will not end then because man is destined to live somewhere forever. Where he spends eternity will be settled by his relationship to the Lord Jesus Christ. The people who have come to Christ and received Him have a bright future before them. One day the Lord will establish His glorious kingdom for which all creation yearns. "Then shall the righteous shine forth as the sun in the kingdom of their Father" (Matt. 13:43).

Fun science project:
Make a pinhole camera by taking a small box (shoebox), drilling a 1/8 inch hole in one end, pasting a sheet of white paper on the inside of the opposite end then aiming it toward the sun. A small image of the sun will shine on the opposite end, complete with sunspots, etc. Never look at the sun itself; it will blind you.

WHO IS SHE THAT LOOKETH FORTH AS THE
MORNING, FAIR AS THE MOON?

SONG OF SOLOMON 6:10

The moon at fourteen days

THE QUEEN OF
THE NIGHT

The moon is the most beautiful of all the celestial objects that can be seen from the earth. We are all familiar with the soft, poetic light that the moon sheds on night scenes. Moonlight has given rise to some of the most famous lines in literature. In the last act of Shakespeare's *The Merchant of Venice,* Lorenzo says to Jessica in the garden, "How sweet the moonlight sleeps upon this bank! / Here will we sit and let the sounds of music / Creep in our ears. Soft stillness and the night / Become the touches of sweet harmony." But one does not have to be a Shakespeare to appreciate the beauty of the moon.

Our only natural satellite, the moon, is close enough and large enough to deserve the title "The Queen of the Night." The moon is 2,160 miles in diameter. Compared to the 7,913 miles of the earth's diameter, that figure does not sound large, but in reality it is an imposing size for a satellite. Most moons are tiny in comparison with the planet that they circle. For example, the two moons of Mars, Phobos and Deimos, are only ten miles and five miles in diameter respectively. Our moon is gigantic compared to them. In comparison with its planet, our moon is proportionally the largest known satellite in our solar system. If one could drop the moon in the Atlantic Ocean, one side of it would touch Europe and the other would touch the North American continent.

The early astronomers thought that the moon was an inhabited globe similar to our earth. The names that they gave to the surface features of the moon show that they thought that the dark portions of the moon were oceans and seas and the lighter portions were continents. Modern photographs show that idea to be in error, for they indicate craters on both the dark and light portions.

The study of the moon's surface is called selenography, from the Greek word for the moon, *selene*. Astronomers have retained the early names for the surface features of the moon even though we know them to be completely different from what the names indicate. One dark area with white spots in it has the Latin name *Mare Nubium* (Sea of Clouds). Another large dark area is called *Oceanus Procellarum* (Ocean of Storms), whereas still another is known as *Mare Imbrium* (Sea of Showers). In a different area are *Mare Serenitatis* (Sea of Serenity) and *Mare Tranquillitatis* (Sea of Tranquility). Of course, not one of these so-called "seas" or "oceans" has a drop of water in it. Astronauts have proved that they are plains of solidified lava. There are also many craters in the "seas" as well as in the upland regions. One great crater with rays radiating from it is named after the astronomer Copernicus; one alongside it is named Kepler after another famous astronomer. A dark crater at the edge of the Sea of Showers is named after the philosopher Plato. Stretching away from Plato is a great mountain range appropriately named the Alps after its earthly counterpart. The mountains and craters of the moon are more rugged in appearance than those on earth because there is no water or atmosphere to erode the jagged outline of the rocks.

The Hebrew word for the moon is *yareach*, which means "wanderer." The name is appropriate, for the moon is never still; it changes its position and its appearance every evening. The psalmist tells us that God "appointed the moon for seasons" (Ps. 104:19). Many ancient peoples based their calendars on the lunar month of approximately 29 days. When the moon is between the earth and the sun, we say that it is a new moon. Since the sun is shining on the opposite side of the moon, we are unable to see the moon at all because only its darkened side is turned toward us.

It actually takes the moon only about 27 days to travel around the earth and back to that same point against the star background. But in that time the earth has moved in its orbit around the sun so that the moon must travel an extra two days in order once again to place itself between the earth and the sun. Thus the exact average lunar month is 29 days, 12 hours, 54 minutes, and 3 seconds.

The moon rises in the east and sets in the west just as the sun and all the stars do. The spinning of the earth on its axis from west to east makes everything in the sky appear to move from east to west. However, since the moon is orbiting the earth from west to east, it appears on each successive evening about 13 degrees farther toward the east. A day or two after the new moon we notice a thin crescent moon low in the western sky immediately after sunset. The whole darkened disk of the moon appears very faintly alongside the crescent. Astronomers call this "the old moon in the new moon's arms." The cause of this unusual appearance is "earthlight," the earth reflecting the light of the sun back to the darkened side of the moon.

As the moon mounts higher in the sky each night, it soon becomes a larger crescent. Seven days after the new moon we can see the first quarter. At this phase one-half of the visible disk of the moon is illuminated by the sun. The term "first quarter" is not a misnomer because one quarter of the total area of the moon is illuminated from our viewpoint. The moon travels on toward the east and waxes into a gibbous, or "humpbacked," moon—the phase between the quarter moon and the full moon. Then about 14 days after the new moon there appears the full moon. At this phase the moon rises at the same time that the sun sets because it is on the opposite side of the earth from the sun. During this phase, the moon is in the sky all night long, setting as the sun rises. After the full phase, the moon wanes to the gibbous phase, the last quarter, the final crescent, and then back to the new moon. This entire cycle astronomers call a lunation or lunar month.

Phases of the moon

The same surface features are visible throughout all the phases of the moon. The reason is that when the moon makes one revolution of its orbit around the earth, it also makes one rotation on its axis, so that it always keeps the same face turned toward the earth. It is possible, however, to see more than one-half of the moon. The moon is in an elliptical, elongated orbit that is closer to the earth on one side than it is on the other. When the moon is on the side closer to the earth, it speeds up; when it is on the side farther from the earth, it slows down. Meanwhile, its rate of rotation on its own axis does not change. This is the result: When the moon is at the apogee, or farthest point from the earth, it is going the slowest. At that same time we can see half the moon along its axis. But it is going so slowly that by the time it has made a quarter turn on its axis, it has traveled only a short distance, and we can see partially around one side. As it comes closer to the earth, it speeds up until at perigee, closest point to the earth, we again see half the moon along its axis. But now its increased speed carries it much farther around by the time that it has made another quarter turn so that we can see more of the other side. Because of this rotation (called the libration of the moon), we can see four-sevenths of the moon's surface instead of just one-half.

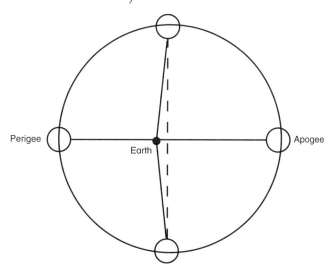

Libration of the moon

The moon in the night sky is certainly an impressive sight. John Milton has described such a scene in *Paradise Lost*:

> . . . now glow'd the Firmament
> With living Sapphires; Hesperus that led
> The starry Host, rode brightest, till the Moon,
> Rising in clouded Majesty, at length
> Apparent Queen unveil'd her peerless light,
> And o'er the dark her Silver Mantle threw.

The moon, with all the other celestial objects, was created by God Himself to manifest His glory to the universe. The first reference to the moon in Scripture is as the "lesser light to rule the night" of the two great lights which God created (Gen. 1:16). The first time the moon is named in Scripture is in the dream of Joseph in which he sees "the sun and the moon and the eleven stars" bowing down to him (Gen. 37:9). The psalmist well exhorts us, "Praise ye the Lord . . . Praise ye him, sun and moon: praise him, all ye stars of light" (Ps. 148:1, 3). But mankind is quick to forget God and to pervert the good gifts of the Lord. Moses strictly warned the children of Israel against such perversion before they entered the promised land, "lest thou lift up thine eyes unto heaven, and when thou seest the sun, and the moon, and the stars, even all the host of heaven, shouldest be driven to worship them" (Deut. 4:19). But the warning of Moses went unheeded. The Israelites worshiped the moon as well as the other objects in the skies, until we are told that King Josiah "put down the idolatrous priests . . . ; them also that burned incense unto Baal, to the sun, and to the moon, and to the planets, and to all the host of heaven" (II Kings 23:5).

However, out of the 61 references in Scripture to the moon, many speak of good things. When God made His covenant with King David, God promised him that "his seed shall endure for ever, and his throne as the sun before me. It shall be established for ever as the moon, and as a faithful witness in heaven" (Ps. 89:36-37). In the Song of Solomon, the bridegroom compliments his bride by saying: "Who is she that looketh forth as the morning, fair as the moon, clear as the sun . . . ?" (6:10).

The prophets looked forward to the glorious reign of the Messiah, and in describing the blessedness of that future day Isaiah says, "Moreover the light of the moon shall be as the light of the sun, and the light of the sun shall be sevenfold, as the light of seven days, in the day that the Lord bindeth up the breach of his people, and healeth the stroke of their wound" (Isa. 30:26). The prophets also saw a time of tribulation and punishment for sin that the world will experience before the restoration of Messiah's reign. The prophet Joel, speaking of the terror of that day, says, "The heavens shall tremble: the sun and the moon shall be dark, and the stars shall withdraw their shining . . . for the day of the Lord is great and very terrible; and who can abide it?" (Joel 2:10-11).

The moon is just close enough to fascinate adventurous men. It seems to be beckoning men to come and explore its rocky craters. The average distance of the moon from the center of the earth is 238,857 miles. A jet pilot who has flown around the world nine times has flown the same distance. The big problem has been to gain enough speed to escape the pull of the earth's gravity. Only recently has scientific technology made possible closer inspection of the moon and also a view of the earth from space. The earth as the astronauts on *Apollo 8* saw it on man's first flight to the moon—its blue oceans and white clouds fully visible—was a splendid sight. Perhaps the best remembered event of *Apollo 8* was the Christmas Eve 1968 television program broadcast back to the earth during which the astronauts read from the first chapter of Genesis: "In the beginning God created the heaven and the earth." It was a most beautiful and fitting way to celebrate man's first journey toward the moon.

From May 18 to May 26, 1969, the astronauts Stafford, Young, and Cernan made a circumlunar flight in *Apollo 10*. During the lunar orbiting, they piloted the lunar module down

to within 9.26 miles of the moon's surface. While the spacecraft orbited the moon, the astronauts had the chance to see a spectacular earthrise. Men sometimes pause on earth to watch the beauty of a moonrise or a sunrise, but these men now had the opportunity to watch the blue and white form of the earth rise above the rugged lunar surface. The grim surface of the moon and the blackness of space presented a striking background for the beautiful pastel colors of the earth as it rose slowly over the moon. But all the activities and observations of *Apollo 10* were simply a preparation for the next moon flight.

On July 16, 1969, *Apollo 11* blasted off into space to attempt the first lunar landing. All the earth waited in suspense as the space flight drew near to the moon. Right on schedule, the lunar module *Eagle* came down for a landing in the Sea of Tranquility. On July 20, 1969, the lunar module landed on the moon. It was a time for rejoicing as man's long dream of exploring the moon was fulfilled.

Some advocates of the theory of evolution had thought that during the long ages of the moon's existence a surface layer of meteoritic dust would have accumulated to such a thickness that an astronaut stepping onto the moon would be in danger of disappearing out of sight. The dust turned out to be a fraction of an inch deep.[1] These advocates of evolution are now in a quandary: where have all the ages of meteoritic dust gone? There is neither wind nor rain to remove it from the moon. At any rate it gave a strange feeling to see the footprints of man on the moon as the astronauts walked about performing the work and experiments they had come to do. For most of us it is more relaxing to view the "Queen of the Night" from a safer distance!

God created the moon to give light upon the earth. Its soft light, so different from that of the brilliant sun, is one of the most pleasant and restful sights on earth. It was God's love for man that caused Him to create the earth and to set it in such a

---

[1] Although apparently there are pockets of deeper dust, the deepest found is inadequate to authenticate evolutionary ages.

beautiful and beneficial relationship to the sun, moon, and stars. The psalmist thinks of this blessing and says, "O give thanks unto the Lord . . . to him that made great lights: for his mercy endureth for ever: the sun to rule by day: for his mercy endureth for ever: the moon and stars to rule by night: for his mercy endureth for ever" (Ps. 136:1, 7-9).

WANDERING STARS
JUDE 13

THE PAGEANT OF
THE PLANETS

When man looks up at the sky, he generally notices objects in the order of their brightness. The brightest of the heavenly bodies are, of course, the sun and moon. The next brightest objects appear to be stars, but they are not. They are the planets. The ancients called them "the wandering stars" because they were continually changing their positions in the sky.

Our sun, as we learned earlier, is a star. Around the sun are nine planets in generally concentric orbits that are really elliptical. Earth is one of the planets. The solar system includes a great many asteroids, comets, meteors, and satellites as well, but the planets command the most attention. In the solar system only the sun shines with its own light; the planets shine by reflecting the sun's light. They are close enough, however, to appear much brighter than most of the stars.

One of the first questions people ask about the planets is how to distinguish them from the stars. The surest way to identify the planets is to be familiar with the positions of the stars and constellations that do not perceptibly change. Then when the bright planets move across this backdrop, they are easily sighted and appear as "the wandering stars."

The planets move along a definite path in the sky. The center of that path is the ecliptic, the apparent path of the sun among the stars. The planets can almost always be found within about eight degrees on each side of the ecliptic. The 12 constellations of the zodiac form the background for the path of the planets.

The planets are mentioned by name only once in Scripture. When the good King Josiah instituted his reforms and started a great revival in Judah, the Bible says that "he put down the idolatrous priests" and "them also that burned incense unto Baal, to the sun, and to the moon, and to the planets, and to all the host of heaven" (II Kings 23:5). It is a sad commentary on the sinfulness of mankind that the only time the planets are named in the Bible, they are portrayed as the objects of idolatrous worship by false teachers.

Although Scripture rarely refers to the planets, references in literature are not scarce. In *Paradise Lost* John Milton, speaking of God's completion of His creation, said,

> The Planets in their stations list'ning stood,
> While the bright Pomp ascended jubilant.
> Open, ye everlasting Gates, they sung,
> Open, ye Heavens, your living doors; let in
> The great Creator from his work return'd.

We shall soon perceive how gracious God was in His creation, for He placed man on the one planet that is ideally suited for him. God has supplied Earth with abundant resources of oxygen and water, which are relatively scarce in the universe. When man ventures forth to explore the other planets, he exchanges a beneficial environment for a dangerous one. The possibility of life on other planets we shall consider as we go along.

Because Mercury is the planet closest to the sun, it is very difficult to see. Most of the time it is lost in the blinding glare of the sun's light. But when Mercury is at its farthest apparent distance from the sun, it can be seen for a few days as a morning star or evening star. But even a number of professional astronomers have complained that it is difficult to see Mercury.

At the relatively close distance of about 36 million miles from the sun, Mercury is able to complete its revolution around the sun in only 88 days. Since it takes 58 days to rotate once on its axis, the days on Mercury are nearly two months long. Because of this slow rotation, the side toward the sun is saturated with flaming heat for months. The Mariner space probes have shown that the daytime temperature on the surface of Mercury is as high as 400° Celsius. Its temperature is certainly hot enough to melt metals such as lead and tin. In contrast, the temperature on the night side of Mercury drops lower than -170° Celsius. The subsurface temperatures are well below freezing in polar regions but above freezing at all times in the equatorial regions. Obviously, Mercury is both too hot and too cold to support life as we know it.

Mercury is the second smallest of the planets, with a diameter of about 3,032 miles. (Pluto is the smallest.) The next planet from the sun, Venus, at a distance of more than 67 million miles from the sun, is closer to the size of Earth. Venus averages about 7,521 miles in diameter compared to the 7,926 miles of Earth's

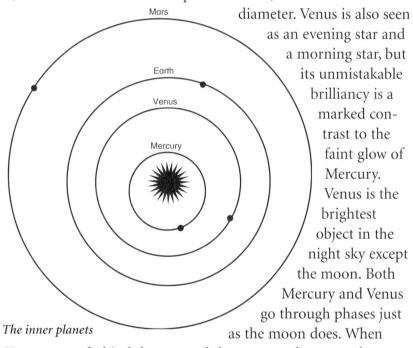

The inner planets

diameter. Venus is also seen as an evening star and a morning star, but its unmistakable brilliancy is a marked contrast to the faint glow of Mercury. Venus is the brightest object in the night sky except the moon. Both Mercury and Venus go through phases just as the moon does. When Venus passes behind the sun and then approaches us as the evening star, it wanes from full to half to crescent phase. As it passes the sun on our side, it goes through the phases again in reverse order. It is brightest in its crescent phase because then it is closest to us.

Venus completes its revolution around the sun in about 225 days. Venus is the planet of mystery. All our observations have shown that we are looking not at the surface of Venus but at a dense covering of clouds that completely hides the surface. These clouds give Venus the highest reflecting power of all the planets, but they certainly obscure our knowledge of the planet. Apparently the clouds have a rotation period of four to six days in a retrograde direction. The surface of Venus is also rotating in a retrograde motion, but at a much slower rate of 243 days. Curiously, the result is that every time Venus is in inferior conjunction between the earth and the sun, it presents the same side to the earth. The latest investigations have indicated the presence of carbon dioxide, carbon monoxide, and water vapor. The carbon dioxide is in such large quantities that it is surely a deadly poison in the atmosphere. The latest investigation reveals that the surface temperature is about 867° F, far too hot for life to exist.

The third planet from the sun is our own earth, which, as we have learned earlier, is approximately 93 million miles from the sun. We rarely think of our earth as a planet hurtling through space with a velocity of 18.5 miles per second as it orbits the sun in 365¼ days. Viewed from the moon, the earth is strikingly beautiful. Because the moon has no atmosphere, scientists there would have an unparalleled view of the universe. Therefore, astronomers want to establish an observatory on the moon. It would be fascinating to watch from the moon the earth rotating on its axis every 23 hours and 56 minutes. There is an interesting reference to the earth in the prophets. Isaiah refers to the Lord God, "It is he that sitteth upon the circle [lit. roundness] of the earth, and the inhabitants thereof are as grasshoppers" (Isa. 40:22). The Hebrew word for "roundness" may well hint at the spherical nature of the earth.

The moon would also provide us a better view of the planet Mars, fourth from the sun at a distance of over 141 million miles. Mars moves around the sun in an orbit of about 687 days. From year to year it may be found anywhere along the ecliptic.

A far more impressive view of Mars than we could get from our moon would be the view from one of Mars' own moons such as Deimos, the outer moon. We would see a small planet of only 4,222 miles diameter that rotates on its axis once every 24 hours and 37 minutes.

There is evidence of an atmosphere on Mars. The polar caps increase during the Martian winter and sometimes disappear completely during the summer. In fact, a band of blue-green spreads out from the polar cap as it melts in the Martian spring. However, the polar caps should not be thought of as vast beds of ice, because the atmosphere is very rare on Mars. In all probability the ice of the polar caps is only a few inches thick. Astronomers have seen the polar caps melt in summer at the rate of 20 miles a day, an occurrence which would be impossible if the ice were very thick.

Mars

From its inner moon, Phobos, Mars would loom gigantic on the horizon, because Phobos is very close to Mars. Circling Mars in only 7 hours and 39 minutes, Phobos would appear from Mars to rise in the west and set in the east. It is the only satellite

Martian panorama from Viking Lander (courtesy NASA)

in the solar system whose period of revolution is faster than the rotation period of its planet.

From Phobos we could get a clear view of the seasons. Some astronomers guess that the green areas on Mars are some form of plant life that spreads as the meager water vapor from the polar ice reaches it. The plants would have to be similar to lichens, which can survive extreme cold and lack of atmosphere. The existence of life on Mars is highly unlikely. Experiments conducted by the Viking Landers have detected carbon dioxide and water on Mars, but none of the more complex carbon compounds. The atmosphere is made up of 95% carbon dioxide plus nitrogen and argon. Photographs sent back to earth show an orange-pink sky.

The reddish areas are apparently vast deserts of iron oxide that give the "red planet" its characteristic color. Is there life on Mars? If by life is meant animal life, most scientists would answer with an unqualified no. The mean temperature on Mars is -85° F, and its atmosphere is as rare as Earth's atmosphere five miles above Mount Everest. Plant life would have to be extremely hardy to survive a climate like that; consequently, most scientists think that the green areas on Mars are caused by something other than plants. The Viking Landers have failed to detect any life on Mars.

One of the most controversial aspects of Mars is the appearance of the so-called canals. Many astronomers deny their very existence because they are so faint that photographs will not record them. When astronomers are watching Mars through a telescope, sometimes the atmosphere seems to clear, and a network of thread-like lines appears for a few seconds; then the atmosphere becomes turbulent again, and the lines fade from view. These tantalizing glimpses have provoked a great deal of speculation, but Viking Lander photographs reveal no canals.

Beyond Mars is the asteroid belt. The asteroids, sometimes called the minor planets, are apparently chunks of rock and metal with very irregular shapes. There are thousands and thousands of them, mainly between the orbits of Mars and Jupiter. The largest one, Ceres, is only about 480 miles in diameter, and most of the others are much, much smaller.

We must go a long way beyond Mars before we come to the orbit of Jupiter, for it averages more than 483 million miles from the sun. Everything about Jupiter seems to need a superlative. It is the largest of the planets, having a diameter averaging about 88,846 miles. It has a large number of natural satellites, 38 moons, revolving around it. The four largest moons can be seen with the aid of a very small telescope. Discovered in 1610 by Galileo, they were the first moons to be identified by a telescope.

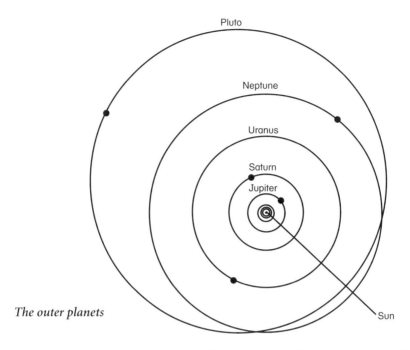

The outer planets

Pluto

Neptune

Uranus

Saturn

Jupiter

Sun

If we could transport ourselves the great distance to one of these moons of Jupiter such as Io, the vast size of Jupiter could be most impressive. The bands of gases and the Great Red Spot could easily be observed. The gases at the equator are moving faster than those nearer the poles. At the equator Jupiter rotates on its axis in 9 hours and 50 minutes, but closer to the poles it takes 9 hours and 55 minutes. This speed of rotation gives Jupiter an oblate appearance.

Jupiter assuredly has an atmosphere, but a most unpleasant one. Astronomers examining Jupiter's dark belts and bright zones have detected both ammonia and methane. Methane is the dreaded marsh gas that has such a deadly effect in coal mines. The only other gas that has been identified is hydrogen. Thus, we can be sure from these poisonous gases that life as we know it does not exist on Jupiter.

The Great Red Spot has been a source of many speculations for over a century and has been carefully observed by

Jupiter

astronomers since about 1831. It is a large oval about 30,000 miles long. At different times it seems to change its longitude as though it were a huge chunk of ice floating in the liquid surface of the planet. Here again, astronomers must admit that they just do not know the real nature of this feature.

Jupiter is one of the most interesting planets for an observer to view from the earth. With a small telescope one can easily see the four largest moons, and a number of amateur astronomers regularly record the varying positions of the moons orbiting around Jupiter. One of the strangest circumstances of Jupiter is the fact that four of the outer moons go around the planet retrograde, a direction opposite to that of the other moons.[1] This is another great puzzle for astronomers.

Both Jupiter and Saturn move very slowly among the constellations of the zodiac. Jupiter takes almost 12 years to complete its orbit around the sun; Saturn requires about 29.5 years. The reason for Saturn's slow pace is its great distance from the sun: more than 890.8 million miles.

The most striking feature of Saturn is its huge ring system. Astronomers estimate that the rings are about 171,000 miles in diameter, though only about ten miles thick. If we could reach the level of the atmosphere on Saturn and look up at the rings, we would see a strange and magnificent sight. The inner ring is faint and hazy, sometimes called the "crepe ring" because it is transparent. The middle ring is the brightest and largest, about 16,000 miles wide. It is separated from the outer ring by the famous Cassini division, named after the astronomer who first detected it through a telescope. Altogether the bands are probably about 41,000 miles wide. They seem to be made up of tiny particles of dust and crystals of ice.

Saturn, like Jupiter, is a giant planet; its average diameter is about 74,897 miles. But because Saturn rotates on its axis so rapidly, in only 10.7 hours, it is about 4,000 miles larger at the equator. This rotation gives the planet a decidedly oval appearance. There are 39 moons orbiting around Saturn.

If we could view Saturn from its largest moon, Titan, we would easily perceive its oval shape. From the distance of Titan, Saturn would dominate the sky and would appear to go through phases just as our moon does. The moon Titan is interesting in itself because it is the only satellite in the entire solar system that is proven to have an atmosphere. Thus, it is the only moon where the sky would appear blue as it does in our atmosphere on Earth. Of course, the atmosphere of Titan also contains poi-

[1] Most recent discovery indicates 38 moons orbiting Jupiter.

Saturn

sonous methane and ammonia that we have found on the larger planets.

One of the unusual characteristics of Saturn is its low density. For all its great size Saturn actually has a density lower than water. If we could just find a body of water large enough, Saturn would float on it!

The planets discussed so far are all visible to the naked eye, but to see the rest of the planets one needs a telescope. The astronomer William Herschel discovered the planet Uranus in 1781. While he was observing certain stars through a telescope, he accidentally saw a green-colored object, which turned out to be Uranus. It is at such a distance from the sun, 1,784,800,000 miles, that it takes Uranus more than 84 years to complete its orbit around the sun. The diameter of Uranus is 31,763 miles. There are 20 moons known to orbit Uranus.

After astronomers had tracked the orbit of Uranus for some years, they realized that something—perhaps another planet farther away from the sun—caused the path of Uranus to be erratic. Two different astronomers calculated where such a planet should be, and in 1846 Neptune was discovered close to the calculated spot.

One would need a very powerful telescope to see Neptune. Moving even more slowly than Uranus, Neptune requires almost 165 years to complete its orbit around the sun. Neptune is another giant planet of about 30,775 miles in diameter.

The same irregularities were detected in Neptune's orbit as in Uranus's. Another planet was suspected, but it was 1930 before Pluto was discovered. Neptune is 2,793,100,000 miles from the sun, but Pluto's average distance is the greatest of all: 3,647,200,000 miles (although Pluto has such an irregular orbit that sometimes it is closer to the sun than is Neptune). Pluto is the smallest of the planets (only 1,485 miles in diameter) and takes more than 248 years to complete its orbit around the sun. Only the greatest telescopes can spot it.

The outer planets are extremely cold. Jupiter is estimated to have a surface temperature of $-166°$ F; Saturn $-220°$ F. The other planets range proportionally down to Pluto, whose temperature is estimated at $-375°$ F. The frigid and poisonous atmospheres on these planets preclude the possibility of life.

God has put man on the most suitable planet in the solar system for him to live. The mere thought of trying to breathe the ammonia on Jupiter instead of oxygen or of seeing rivers of molten lead on Mercury instead of life-sustaining water makes vivid to us the grace and love of our Creator.

THE STARS OF HEAVEN FELL UNTO THE EARTH

REVELATION 6:13

VISITORS FROM OUTER SPACE

The thought of visitors from outer space conjures up a picture of little green men climbing out of their flying saucer. Most people are interested in whether there is intelligent life besides our own in the universe. Recognized authorities are posing the question in books with such titles as *Life Beyond Our Planet* (Dan Posin), *Is There Life on Other Worlds?* (Poul Anderson), and, more bluntly still, *Is Anybody Out There?* (John Rublowsky). The difficulties in trying to investigate such a subject are immense. Man's instruments are barely strong enough to detect the existence of planets going around any other star, much less the existence of intelligent life on them. The Christian position does not deny that there may be life anywhere else, but rather maintains that if there is life anywhere else, God created it. Life does not spontaneously evolve. The only physical life that we can be sure exists is the life here on planet Earth.

We shall not, therefore, speculate idly about the existence of life elsewhere in the universe or about UFOs but rather discuss the very factual visits of such things as meteorites and comets to our part of the universe. It is easy to prove that meteors are striking our atmosphere in such quantities that tons of meteoritic dust are sifting down to the surface of the earth every day.

When a truly great comet appears in the night sky, men stop to view the awesome sight. But since only two or three comets in an average five-year period are visible to the unaided eye, most comets are not seen by amateur observers. For the same reason very few meteorites are observed in falling. Yet astronomers estimate that there are billions upon billions of meteoroids and comets orbiting around the sun in our solar system.

A meteor is the flash of light in the night sky popularly called a shooting star. A meteoroid is the chunk of stony or metallic matter that strikes our atmosphere causing the flash of light. If the meteoroid gets all the way down to the surface of the earth, it is called a meteorite. There are three kinds of meteorites: stony meteorites, iron meteorites, and stony-iron meteorites. The iron meteorites are easy to identify because of their heavy weight, but there are many more stony meteorites that fall to the earth. After a few years, however, a stony meteorite weathers until it looks much like any other rock to the untrained observer.

As astronomers continually map the stars of the night sky on photographic plates, they often quite accidentally discover some visitor from outer space. The streak of a meteor will appear on some photographs; on others a small blurred patch of light will appear. Whenever an astronomer sees such a patch of light, he takes another photograph to see if the patch has moved among the background stars. If it has moved, he concludes that it is another comet. When he has three different sightings of the comet, he notifies Harvard Observatory, which acts as the clearing house for all identifications of comets in this country. If no one else has spotted that comet, it will be named for the astronomer who first notified the observatory. The comet Kohoutek received its name from a Czech astronomer working at the Hamburg Observatory in West Germany who was the first to photograph it. When astronomers calculated the orbit of comet Kohoutek, they found that it would come within 13 million miles of the sun—much nearer than the average comet. It was quickly called "the comet of the century." Some astronomers prophesied that it would be brighter than the moon in the night sky. As everyone now knows, comet Kohoutek pulled one of the best disappearing comet acts in history. Such a large telescopic lens was required to see Kohoutek that most people saw absolutely nothing of it.

Plainly, comets may be unpredictable. A number of mysteries about comets puzzle the best astronomers. Let us survey the things we do know about these mysterious visitors from outer space.

Out of some 571 individual comets whose orbits have been calculated, 215 are periodic comets that are expected to return to the sun, whereas 356 will not return again. Of the 215 periodic comets, 121 are long-period comets whose orbits will take 200 years or more to complete, and 94 are short-period comets whose orbits are less than 200 years.[1] Most short-period comets have orbits that take only six or seven years to complete. Only one in ten comets is bright enough to be seen on a second passage of the sun.[2]

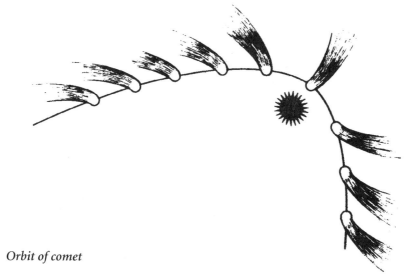

Orbit of comet

Sometimes a close passage of even a large comet to the sun causes the comet to break up. Such was the fate of the great comet of 1861. Every year from August 10 to 14 the earth passes through the orbit of that comet, but it has not been seen again.

[1] Nikolaus B. Richter, *The Nature of Comets,* trans. Arthur Beer (London: Menthuen, 1963), p. 9.

[2] J. H. Oort, "Empirical Data on the Origins of Comets." *The Moon, Meteorites, and Comets,* eds. Barbara M. Middlehurst and Gerard P. Kuiper (Chicago: Univ. of Chicago Press, 1963), p. 670.

During those dates we do see the Perseid meteor shower. Astronomers have proved that about a half dozen of the major meteor showers are the result of the breakup of a comet. No meteorite, however, has ever been observed to fall from a meteor shower. Some astronomers think, because of this fact, that comets are made up mostly of ice crystals with very little solid matter to burn up in the earth's atmosphere. In the great meteor shower of 1833, the meteors were described as falling as thick as snowflakes, hundreds being visible every second. Yet not one meteorite was recovered.

Comet Arend-Roland

What do we know about the structure of a comet? When a comet is very far out in space away from the sun, it has a solid nucleus. Apparently the nucleus is made up of ice crystals formed from cyanogen, methane, ammonia, and other gases mixed with dust and small bits of matter. This solid nucleus may be only one or two miles in diameter. Even great comets may have a nucleus only ten miles in diameter. When a comet approaches the sun, ultraviolet radiation vaporizes the ices on the surface of the comet. Though the nucleus is only a few miles in diameter, the head, or coma, of the comet may be 100,000 miles or more in diameter. As the radiation from the sun continues to bombard the comet, the gases begin to trail behind the comet, forming a long tail. The tail of a great comet may be 100 million miles long or more. The gases are spread out so thinly that stars may be seen through the comet's tail, just as clearly as if the tail were not there. The dust tail is relatively short and is spread out at a much greater angle than the gas tail, which is almost always longer and straighter.

Astronomers are not agreed on what kind of mechanism keeps the comet glowing. Apparently the radiation from the sun is not an adequate explanation. Nor does it explain why the molecules of gases are more highly ionized in the center of the coma than they are at the outside.[3] Astronomers are agreed that the direction of the comet's tail—always away from the sun—is a result of the continual radiation pressure from the sun (often called the solar wind). When a comet approaches the sun, its tail trails behind it; as the comet swings around the sun, its tail is always aimed away from the sun; and as the comet recedes from the sun, it always goes away tail first.

Intensive investigation is going on about comets. Astronomers would like to know why (and how) a comet can flare up with a burst of illumination, increasing in brightness as much as

[3] Raymond A. Lyttleton, *Mysteries of the Solar System* (Oxford: Clarendon Press, 1968), p. 143.

six magnitudes in 24 hours.[4] So far there is not even a good guess, much less a reasonable explanation, for such a burst. Astronomers would also like to know why some comets will dim and diminish in light as they approach the sun, rather than increase in brilliance as most comets do. Of course, astronomers would like to be able to explain why the comet Kohoutek failed to brighten at all.

The investigation is continuing. It is the comet watcher's dream to see that faint patch of light on the photographic plate. Relatively few astronomers can afford the time to conduct a comet watch, systematically mapping the stars to find new comets. Most comets are discovered by accident while the astronomer is really hunting for something else. In fact, many comets are discovered by amateurs, because astronomers are too busy with other interests. Some comets have actually become bright enough to be seen with the unaided eye before being noticed by the professionals, who were busy looking in other directions.

When a large comet appears bright enough to be seen with the unaided eye, everyone takes notice. The year 1957 was a banner one for that phenomenon. Two comets bright enough to be seen by anyone appeared. Comet Arend-Roland was an impressive sight. The first detail that caught everyone's attention was the so-called "anti-tail" that appeared to be aimed at the sun. It soon became apparent that this was an optical illusion caused by perspective. Both tails were aimed away from the sun, but they were at about a 100° angle to one another.[5] Our viewing position on the earth made it look as though one tail was pointed at the sun. Comet Arend-Roland was a dust comet; that is, it had a large amount of dust in it.[6] The thin spike of the anti-tail was the dust tail. The dust was spread out along a very thin plane.

[4] Fred L. Whipple, "On the Structure of the Cometary Nucleus," *The Moon, Meteorites, and Comets*, p. 652.

[5] Richter, pp. 101-5.

[6] Ibid., p. 116.

The gas tail was a much fatter, more normal-looking tail. In reality, however, the dust tail was somewhat longer than the gas tail. The unusual appearance of comet Arend-Roland aroused great interest, and many astronomers paused in their other work to investigate it. One of the interesting facts discovered was that the light coming from comet Arend-Roland was strongly polarized. In fact, the polarization was about equivalent to that of an iron meteorite.[7] This feature raises the question of whether comet Arend-Roland has a large sandbank of solid particles mixed in with the ice crystals. Astronomers are by no means agreed on the interpretation of all this data. Obviously, the investigations must continue.

The other bright comet of 1957 was Mrkos. It also had more than one tail. The dust tail was spread out on both sides of the longer, thinner gas tail. One surprising detail about the comet Mrkos was the obvious smoke ring in the gas tail. The tails of comets change in their appearance daily, so that such features often disappear within 24 hours. Investigation of comet Mrkos revealed that its tail was about 42 million kilometers long. Photoelectric measurements also showed that comet Mrkos was slightly polarized.

In 1961 the comet Humason was discovered. Photographs by the Mount Palomar Observatory showed a contorted appearance of the tail. Continuing observations showed that the tail had a very ragged appearance. On one occasion a considerable portion of the tail was completely detached from the nucleus of the comet.[8] It is not very clear what is happening to the tail. All that astronomers can do is record their observations with great care and hope that continuing study will reveal some explanations for such unusual appearances.

Normally about every three years a comet shows up that is bright enough to be seen with the unaided eye. In 1970 another such comet, the comet Bennett, appeared. It turned out to be a

[7] Ibid., p. 113.

[8] Ibid., p. 92.

good comet for amateurs to observe and photograph. Most comets that are observed are seen by people who have highly specialized equipment for detecting them. Of course, most

Comet Ikeya-Seki

comets are not seen by anyone because they do not come near enough to the sun to become bright enough to be seen. Sometimes a comet that is too faint to be seen until the light of the sun is blotted out is discovered during a total eclipse of the sun. Only about three or four times in a century does a comet appear that is bright enough to be seen in the daylight sky.

In 1965 one of these rare daylight comets appeared. It was the great comet Ikeya-Seki, the first daylight comet to be seen since 1927. The long, sharply defined tail beamed like a searchlight against the night sky. Comet Ikeya-Seki belongs to a group of comets that are called the "sun-grazing comets." They come very close to the sun and often become very bright. Sometimes the comets that come very close to the sun break up into more than one comet; some disintegrate completely and are not seen again. The great daylight comet of 1882 broke up into five different comets.[9]

Halley's comet is the most famous of all the comets. It keeps coming back on an average of every 76 years. The first recorded

[9] Lyttleton, p. 122.

sighting was in 240 B.C., when Chinese astronomers described the great comet that appeared. Since the ancient peoples regarded comets as a portent of great disaster such as war, pestilence, or famine, the appearance of Halley's comet in A.D. 66 was regarded as foreshadowing the coming fall of Jerusalem. It appeared at the Battle of Hastings in 1066. Although it was impressive in 1910, its last return in 1986 was rather dim. Astronomers look for its return in 2062.

Comets travel with a continually changing speed. The farther away from the sun that the comet is, the slower it is traveling; the nearer to the sun it is, the faster it is traveling. A periodic comet such as Halley's travels in an elliptical orbit. When the comet is farthest from the sun, it is traveling very slowly. As it moves in toward the sun past the orbit of the planet Neptune, it begins picking up speed. The comet passes the orbit of Uranus and the orbits of Saturn and Jupiter, continually increasing in its speed. When it swings around the sun, it is traveling the fastest. As it moves on out away from the sun, it slows down.

One of the most spectacular visitors from outer space was the Tunguska meteorite that fell in Siberia on June 30, 1908. Everything within a radius of 18 kilometers from the point of the fall was burned; all the trees were torn up by the roots and laid out flat in a radial pattern within 40 kilometers; 60 kilometers away from the fall a man sitting on his porch was knocked unconscious by the shock of the explosion.[10] What puzzled the investigators the most was that there was no crater left by the explosion. Astronomers now think it was the head of a small comet that struck the Tunguska region. Such a head would contain no great blocks of stone to form a crater. It would consist of ice particles and dust particles—perhaps millions of tons of particles. The explosion would be staggering, but there would be no solid matter to form a crater. It was very fortunate that the object fell in such an uninhabited place as Siberia; otherwise, the loss of life would have been a disaster indeed.

[10] E. L. Krinkov, "The Tunguska and Sikhote-Alin Meteorites," *The Moon, Meteorites, and Comets,* pp. 208-18.

A real meteorite formed the Barringer Crater in Arizona. The impact explosion formed a crater about three quarters of a mile in diameter. Astronomers estimate that the meteorite was probably about 200 feet in diameter when it struck. The explosion so shattered it that only fragments have been found. They are spread out for miles around the crater.

The Bible tells of such occurrences yet to come. The Book of Revelation, describing the events of the tribulation period, says that "the stars of heaven fell unto the earth, even as a fig tree casteth her untimely figs, when she is shaken of a mighty wind" (Rev. 6:13). In Greek usage the word *star* often meant "shooting star," or meteor. Apparently this passage describes a mighty meteor shower. Another passage tells us that when the second angel sounded his trumpet, "as it were a great mountain burning with fire was cast into the sea" (Rev. 8:8). The result was that a third of the creatures in the sea died and a third of the ships were destroyed. "A great mountain burning with fire" is an apt description of a great meteorite or a small asteroid entering our atmosphere. If such an object did strike in one of the oceans, it could easily produce tidal waves of 600 to 1,000 feet high. The destruction that such tidal waves could cause can hardly be imagined.

If such events make the future sound forbidding, the Bible also gives a strong hope for the future. But it gives such a hope only to those who know the Lord Jesus Christ as their personal Savior. He is coming again to receive His own people unto Himself. The Epistle of First Thessalonians tells us that the Lord Jesus will call His born-again saints into His presence before the sudden destruction of the tribulation period comes upon this world. No one knows when that day will come. All must be ready for the coming of the Lord Jesus Christ. If He should return today, would He find you ready?

HE . . . STRETCHETH OUT THE HEAVENS AS A CURTAIN

ISAIAH 40:22

M 31 in Andromeda

AN ISLAND UNIVERSE:
THE MILKY WAY GALAXY

On clear evenings the Milky Way stretches like a blurred and irregular path of light across the night sky. The path of light is the edge of our home galaxy. It has even given its name to the galaxy, for ours is known as the Milky Way Galaxy. Over a number of centuries it has had this name. John Milton in *Paradise Lost* speaks of

> ... the Galaxy, that Milky way
> Which nightly as a circling Zone thou seest
> Powder'd with Stars.

Our galaxy is of such a size that it is often called an "island universe." In fact, the early astronomers thought that it was the universe, but modern instruments have shown that the Milky Way Galaxy is just one of countless numbers of galaxies spread out through space so vast that perhaps no one can imagine just how large the universe actually is.

Charles Messier (1730-1817), a famous French astronomer whose main goal in life was discovering comets, is best known today for his catalogue of astronomical objects, the *Messier Catalogue of Nebulae and Star Clusters,* first published in 1771. He made this list of star clusters and nebulae to avoid confusing them with the comets he was trying to find. In the course of his lifetime, he discovered 15 comets; his lasting fame, however, rests on his catalogue, a list of 103 astronomical objects, which are still referred to by their Messier numbers.

Among the spectacular objects that Messier discovered are several galaxies. For example, in the constellation Canes Venatici, the Hunting Dogs, near the last star in the handle of the Big Dipper is a beautiful spiral galaxy, the famous Whirlpool Galaxy,

Messier 51 (or M 51) in the catalogue. It is one of the most perfect spirals among the galaxies and has a smaller satellite galaxy connected with it. A galaxy such as this one may well have 100 billion stars in it, all circling around the central nucleus. M 64, the famous Black Eye Galaxy, in the constellation Coma Berenices, is also a spiral galaxy. Clouds of gas and dust produce an obscuring effect that does look remarkably like a black eye. This galaxy is also made up of billions of stars.

M 51 Whirlpool Galaxy

In the autumn sky can be noticed the great spiral galaxy in the constellation Andromeda, which is identified as M 31. This is another galaxy like our own Milky Way Galaxy, made up of more than 100 billion stars. The stars in the spiral arms of the galaxy are a hot blue, whereas the stars in the central nucleus are mostly a cooler yellow and red. M 31 is a sister galaxy, relatively close to our own.

The constellation just below Andromeda, Triangulum, has another beautiful spiral galaxy, M 33. Although this galaxy is not as large as the one in Andromeda, it is fully as beautiful. It too is made up of billions of stars and is relatively close to our own galaxy. As astronomers phrase it, it is part of the Local Group.

Unfortunately, the galaxies in the northern hemisphere are so far from us that they are very difficult to see without a telescope. In the southern hemisphere are some galaxies close enough to be seen easily by the unaided eye. One such galaxy is

Larger Magellanic Cloud

the Larger Magellanic Cloud, so called because it was first seen by Europeans on Magellan's famous voyage of discovery in 1516-19. This Larger Magellanic Cloud is quite close to our own Milky Way Galaxy. Although it is much smaller than ours, astronomers have still been able to detect star clusters, clouds of luminous gas, double stars, and other features that are found in our own galaxy. One astronomer has said that if the stars were the size of pinheads, the nearest one would still be 100 miles away; but if whole galaxies were the size of pinheads, they would average a mere handbreadth away from one another. The Magellanic Clouds are probably satellite galaxies closely connected to our own.

In order to understand the size of our Milky Way Galaxy, we must use the term *light-year*. Light, which travels at the rate of more than 186,000 miles a second, can travel a distance of more than seven times around the world in just one second. It is staggering to think that light must travel at that speed for 100,000 years in order to pass from one edge of our Milky Way Galaxy to the other. The galaxy is only about 10,000 light-years thick because it has the shape of a great flat pinwheel of stars.

When we look up at the night sky, we are looking out from the inside of the galaxy, and, consequently, it is difficult to perceive the structure of the galaxy. But if we could look down upon it from the outside, we would see the flat side of a great spiral galaxy. Our sun is located near the edge in one of the spiral arms. But the sun is proportionally so small that it could not be seen at all from any distance outside the galaxy.

Human life seems very small when we consider how many billions of galaxies are spread out through space. Light, which travels from the sun to our earth in eight minutes, takes 4.3 years to reach the closest star in our galaxy. Light from our sun takes 27,000 years to reach the center of our galaxy. To reach other spiral galaxies it would take millions of years. Our imagination fails at the thought of such vast distances.

When we think of the vastness of the universe, we are reminded of the power and majesty of our great Creator. The prophet Isaiah said that God "stretcheth out the heavens as a curtain, and spreadeth them out as a tent to dwell in" (Isa. 40:22). We seem to hear the challenge of the prophet Isaiah: "Lift up your eyes on high, and behold who hath created these things, that bringeth out their host by number: he calleth them all by names by the greatness of his might, for that he is strong in power; not one faileth. . . . Hast thou not known? hast thou not heard, that the everlasting God, the Lord, the Creator of the ends of the earth, fainteth not, neither is weary? there is no searching of his understanding" (Isa. 40:26, 28).

When we look at the Milky Way, we are looking past so many stars that the sky is hazy with their light. In the great telescopes the Milky Way can be resolved into individual stars. Many of these stars in the Milky Way are grouped together in most beautiful and interesting combinations. In the faint constellation Canes Venatici between the Big Dipper and Boötes is a beautiful star cluster, but, unfortunately, one needs a powerful telescope to see it. This is the famous globular cluster M 3. The globular clusters get their names from their globe-like shape. They consist of dense concentrations of stars that may number anywhere from 10,000 to a million.

These globular clusters are found all around the Milky Way Galaxy and form a great halo of clusters that surround our galaxy in a spherical shape. The center of one great sphere of globular clusters is in the constellation Sagittarius. The latest investigations of the great radio telescopes confirm that the center of our galaxy lies in the direction of Sagittarius. It is also the spot where the Milky Way appears the brightest, for this is the dense central nucleus of the galaxy. In fact, the radio telescopes have identified a number of the spiral arms of our galaxy that curve out from the central nucleus. Our own sun is located near the inner edge of the Carina-Cygnus arm, so named because it stretches all the way from the constellation Cygnus to the southern constellation Carina. A spur of this arm extends into the constellation Orion. The structure of the galaxy is a subject of intense study because new information is continually coming from the radio telescopes.

Astronomers estimate that our sun is moving in an orbit around the galactic nucleus at a speed of about 140 miles per second. Even though the sun has such a high rate of speed, the distance around the galaxy is so great that it would take our sun more than 200 million years to complete one orbit. This time measurement is often called the galactic year.

Some star clusters seem to spread out along the plane of the galaxy. These are called open clusters because of their open, or spread-out, appearance. The most famous of the open clusters is the Pleiades, which appears among the winter stars. The open clusters are found predominantly along the path of the Milky Way. Astronomers also notice the nebulosity, the clouds of dust and gas, which surround these stars.

Dust and gas comprise an important part of the Milky Way Galaxy. In fact, astronomers estimate that the quantity of dust and gas in the galaxy is equal to the mass of all the stars in the galaxy, but, of course, this quantity of dust and gas is spread out very thinly. A sphere of space the size of our earth would contain about seven pounds of gas. This quantity amounts to a more perfect vacuum than scientists can manufacture in the laboratory.

Some interesting combinations of dust and gas are found in the so-called planetary nebulae. One of the best known is the Ring Nebula in the constellation Lyra the Lyre. The word *nebula* is simply the Latin word for "cloud"; the nebulae are clouds of dust and gas. The planetary nebulae have nothing to do with planets. They were given this description because in the early telescopes they appeared like small disks similar to the shape of the planets.

A faint blue star at the center of the Ring Nebula is pouring out of itself a cloud of luminous gas. Although the cloud looks like a ring, it is actually a complete sphere of gas and dust that surrounds the star on all sides. Spectroscopic studies have revealed that hydrogen, oxygen, and nitrogen are the major gases that we see glowing. The mystery of this Ring Nebula is that the cloud never diminishes. Apparently the star is continually replenishing the cloud with more gas and dust. The Ring Nebula is a favorite target for amateur astronomers because it can be seen with even a small telescope, but it takes a powerful one indeed to record it in color.

Another unusual appearance in the galaxy is a supernova, a star that explodes with tremendous violence. A supernova may become 100 million times brighter than our sun. In the year A.D. 1054 Chinese astronomers recorded in their star charts the appearance of a nova, or new star, which rapidly became the brightest star in the sky. After a few months, it gradually faded from view. The place where the Chinese astronomers saw this new star was a conspicuous location in the constellation Taurus the Bull. Today when modern astronomers train their great telescopes on this spot in the sky, they see the famous Crab Nebula, which is all that is left from the explosion of this supernova. The terrible violence of the explosion is still apparent from the agitated clouds of dust and gas that are streaming away from the

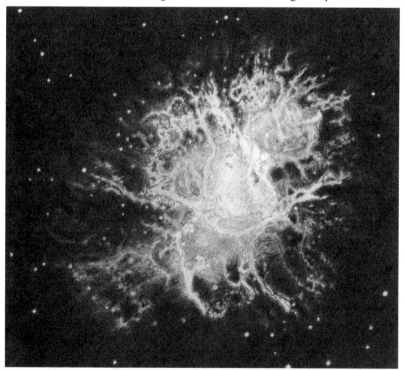

Crab Nebula

star in the center. The star literally blew itself apart, and all that we can now see is the strange and beautiful Crab Nebula that surrounds the much-weakened star.

The vast quantities of dust and gas are not spread out evenly in the Milky Way Galaxy, but are rather often clumped together into clouds, which astronomers call the diffuse nebulae. They are among the most beautiful objects in the entire universe. The most famous of the diffuse nebulae is the Great Cloud Nebula in Orion, which surrounds one of the stars in the "sword" that hangs down from Orion's "belt." Whereas the planetary nebulae were clouds that surround one star, this nebula is large enough to envelop many stars.

Astronomers are acquainted with many clouds of dust and gas in our galaxy, but not all of them are bright clouds. Some are the so-called dark nebulae. One of the best known of the dark nebulae, near the Belt of Orion, is the Horsehead Nebula, a

Horsehead Nebula

cloud of dust and gas that is similar to the Great Nebula in Orion but has no stars in it or near enough to it to illuminate the cloud. Consequently, we see it in silhouette against the light of the background stars. We can see a few stars on our side of the nebula, but obviously it is blotting out the light of the stars behind it.

Sights such as these originated the idea that there were "holes" among the stars and, more particularly, that there was a "hole" among the stars in the north where God's throne was located. Of course, in the early telescopes these dark nebulae did look like "holes" among the stars, but with our much more powerful modern instruments we can perceive that they are clouds of dust and gas that simply do not have any stars near enough to light them up.

Sometimes light and dark nebulae occur in the same area of the sky. One of the best known examples is the North American Nebula in the constellation Cygnus the Swan. In this case it is a dark nebula that forms the outline of the Atlantic Ocean, the Gulf of Mexico, and the Pacific Ocean. The continent itself is formed by a bright nebula. The dark clouds are closer to us than the bright clouds and appear silhouetted against the bright. This is the cause of the familiar continental shape. There are a number of other such combinations of nebulae in our Milky Way Galaxy.

Many of these light and dark clouds have very unusual appearances. One of these formations in the constellation Sagittarius is the so-called Trifid Nebula, M 20. It is a bright cloud of gas and dust that has some narrow bands of dark clouds in front of it. This effect does give the Trifid Nebula a very mysterious appearance. Certainly God's great creation is filled with objects of beauty and variety.

The Milky Way Galaxy is an impressive location for man's planet, the earth. The immensity of the galaxy should cause man to look up and consider his Maker. "For the invisible things of him from the creation of the world are clearly seen, being understood by the things that are made, even his eternal power and Godhead" (Rom. 1:20). The vastness and complexity of the galaxy demands the First Cause. Only a divine Creator is an adequate explanation for such a galaxy. Impersonal force cannot explain design and loving provision. God has designed the universe to provide for mankind and all the rest of His creation an adequate place in which to live.

AND GOD SAID, LET THERE BE LIGHT:
AND THERE WAS LIGHT

GENESIS 1:3

COLOR IN
THE SKY

On the first day of creation God said, "Let there be light: and there was light" (Gen. 1:3). Thus light is older than man. But the creation of light meant the creation of color, for in ordinary white light are all the colors of the rainbow. When light passes through a prism, it is refracted into that rainbow band of color which scientists call the spectrum. Light contains within itself every color. An object that reflects one color will look that color; an object that reflects all colors will look white; one that does not reflect any color will look black. Thus a red rose is not really red; it simply absorbs all other colors and reflects red. A white rose is one that reflects all colors: a black tulip is a flower that absorbs all colors and reflects none.

God, who created such a universe, certainly appreciates beautiful colors. Perhaps this appreciation of color is part of the divine nature, for the New Testament teaches that "God is light" (I John 1:5). When God gave Moses instructions for the building of the tabernacle, He commanded him to make it with boards overlaid with gold and with hangings and curtains of finely woven linen, colored blue, purple, and scarlet (Exod. 26:29-31). God intended man to enjoy the colors, for the Apostle Paul reminds us that God "giveth us richly all things to enjoy" (I Tim. 6:17).

The Scriptures also reveal to us that color is not limited to the physical realm; the spiritual abode of God in heaven is filled with even more splendid colors. When the prophet Ezekiel saw the vision of the four living creatures, he said that they sparkled "like the colour of burnished brass. . . . Over their heads was the likeness of a throne, as the appearance of a sapphire stone." The divine Presence seated upon the throne was "as the colour of amber, as the appearance of fire round about within it." The prophet concluded by saying, "As the appearance of the bow that is in the cloud in the day of rain, so was the appearance of the brightness round about. This was the appearance of the likeness of the glory of the Lord" (Ezek. 1:7, 26-28).

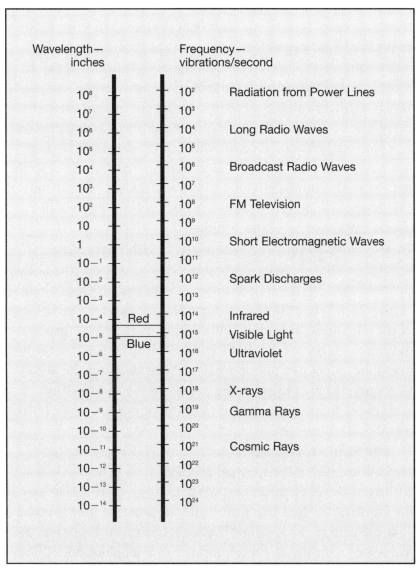

The electromagnetic spectrum

The spiritual realm may afford far greater sensitivity to color than man now has. At the present all that man can perceive of the great spectrum of electromagnetic energy is the one octave known as visible light. But there are sixty octaves of electromagnetic energy. Below the blue of visible light are five octaves of ultraviolet light that are invisible to man; below these are the X-rays, gamma rays, and cosmic rays, all unseen by man. Above the red of visible light are nine octaves of infrared light; above these are the short electromagnetic waves, radar waves, short radio waves, and long radio waves, again all invisible to man. It is not unreasonable to think that the saints in glorified resurrection bodies will be able to perceive the whole spectrum of all sixty octaves of electromagnetic energy and perhaps other splendors that we cannot now even imagine.

Many of the stars have distinctive colors; some of the planets and satellites have bright colors; often the clouds of dust and gas known as nebulae have remarkable colors; and even whole galaxies shine with beautiful colors.

It is surprising how much astronomers have been able to discover from starlight. They have found that the color of the stars is a good indication of their temperature. Just as metal that is heated in fire will begin to glow red, and as the temperature rises will turn orange, yellow, white, and finally a blue-white, so the bluer a star is the hotter it is. The temperature of the stars is usually listed by the Kelvin scale; this is the absolute temperature scale, equivalent to the centigrade scale plus 273°.

The stars classified as "O" are very blue and very hot, about 50,000 kelvins in their surface temperature. "B" stars are blue with a surface temperature of 25,000 kelvins; "A" stars are sometimes green, sometimes white, with a surface temperature of about 11,000 K; "F" stars are white, at about 7,600 K; "G" stars are yellow, at about 6,000 K; "K" stars are orange, at about 5,000 K; and stars classified as "M," "R," "N,"and "S" are red and may have a surface temperature as cool as 3,000 K. Our own sun is plainly a yellow star, which astronomers classify as a "G" star.

Modern instruments such as the spectroscope have added much to our information. The spectroscope is a glass prism or diffraction grating that breaks the light from the stars into the familiar rainbow-band of color known as a spectrum. Each type of star has a distinctive spectrum, formed by the presence of the various chemical elements in it. Many of the elements are in a highly ionized state because of the high temperatures and pressures in the stars.

In the night sky we can view several of these colorful stars. For example, Rigel, in the winter constellation Orion, is a very hot, blue star; Betelgeuse is a cooler, reddish star. Next to Orion in Taurus the Bull, Aldebaran is a bright orange star. Capella, the brightest star in the constellation Auriga, is yellow, as is Pollux in the constellation Gemini the Twins. Arcturus, in Boötes the Herdsman, is a beautiful yellow-orange star. In Virgo the Virgin, Spica is a hot blue-white star; and the brightest star in Lyra the Lyre, Vega, is a true white star. Two other white stars in that area are Altair, in Aquila the Eagle, and Deneb, in Cygnus the Swan. One of the most brilliant stars is in Scorpius, Antares, a great red giant of a star. These are just a few of the most strikingly colorful stars that can be seen without a telescope; there are many, many others.

Besides being able to break down this star light, scientists can also use the spectroscope to tell whether stars are approaching the earth or going away from the earth. When a star is coming towards the earth, the bands in the spectrum are shifted toward the blue end of the spectrum; when it is going away from the earth, they are shifted toward the red end. This observation has led to the discovery of many binary stars. These are stars that orbit around one another. Many of them, however, are so far away from us that even in the greatest telescopes they still appear as one star. We know differently, for periodically their spectra will change. When the pair of stars is moving crossways to our line of sight, they produce a normal spectrum; but when the pair is so turned that one star is approaching us and the other is going away, the lines of the spectrum split, because the light from the star going away is shifted toward the red, whereas the light from the star coming toward us is shifted toward the blue. Of the some 40,000 spectroscopic binary stars, many are in multiple binary systems with whole groups of stars orbiting around one another. As one can imagine, some of the most interesting examples of color among the stars are the combinations of colors in some of the double stars. Close to the yellow Capella in the constellation Auriga is the star Zeta Aurigae. It is a combination of a super-giant red star and a smaller blue-white star. Of course, they are so far away from us that the two appear as one star to the unaided eye.

Each of the planets around our own star, the sun, has its own color characteristics. Earth is filled with color from the iridescent colors on a butterfly's wing to the spectacular forms of the Northern Lights. Scientists hope that close-up photographs of the planet Mars by the Viking Landers will determine why the red planet has areas of blue-green at certain seasons. The planet Jupiter is so far away that scientists do not have much hope of securing accurate color photographs of its surface. Yet scientists are more curious about Jupiter than about other planets because of its mysterious Great Red Spot.

One of the most astonishing displays of color visible to man is the aurora borealis, or the Northern Lights. This pageantry is caused by an unusual phenomenon. Although our sun is continually emitting radiation, when a large sunspot appears a great number of charged particles flare out from the sun's surface. These particles come in a spiral path toward the earth, following the lines of the earth's magnetic field, and, since the earth acts as a great magnet, the particles come into our atmosphere a short distance away from the magnetic north and south poles. When these particles strike the atoms and molecules of the gases in the upper atmosphere, they excite these gases and cause them to glow in the familiar forms of the Northern Lights.

Scientists investigated the Northern Lights for many years before they discovered that the gases causing the aurora were mostly nitrogen and oxygen. The reason the scientists were so long in identifying them was that the gases were in a highly ionized state because of the bombardment with charged particles. This explanation seems obvious enough now, but at the time the scientists were trying to identify the gases it was very difficult to reproduce their spectrum in the laboratory.

Since the aurora is connected with the sunspots, it is also directly connected with the time cycles of the sunspots. If an aurora is very bright, it can often be seen again 27 days later, because the sun rotates on its axis in a 27-day period and the sunspots that caused the aurora are again aimed at the earth. In

Aurora: a rayed band

the same way the aurora follows an 11-year cycle just as the sunspots do. There is a climax in the number and intensity of sunspots every 11 years, and at this time the aurora is also larger and more intense.

Most of the auroral displays are about 65 to 70 miles above the surface of the earth. The highest of the Northern Lights are as much as 640 miles above the earth, whereas the lowest can extend down to 40 miles above the earth. The aurora is actually a great wall of light standing on its edge. Some auroras may be only a half mile high; others may be 85 miles high. They are almost always much longer than they are high; in fact, auroras that extend for hundreds of miles are relatively frequent. One of the largest of the auroras was estimated to be 3,000 miles long. A number of records of auroras show them extending for over 1,000 miles. The height of the aurora varies with the ocean tides. When the moon or sun pulls the atmosphere higher, the Northern Lights will appear at a higher altitude. The brightest displays, however, are at a lower altitude because, the atmosphere being denser there, the sun's particles can affect more atoms and molecules.

The auroras may assume a great variety of forms. Scientists usually classify them as homogeneous bands, homogeneous arcs, rayed arcs, flashing or pulsating auroras, red patches, draperies, rays, rayed bands, or a corona, which is a great sunburst effect. There are many other forms that defy classification. Often the aurora will change rapidly from one form to another so that in the course of one evening a whole series of forms may be seen. The best latitude at which to see such a display is that of central Canada, Alaska, and Greenland. The auroras can be seen as far south as South Carolina, but usually these displays are very faint and very low on the horizon.

The most common color in the aurora is a greenish-yellow, but there may be a wide variety in the colors of a display. There are blue auroras, green auroras, red auroras, and very remarkable combinations of colors, even including lavender and pink. The shimmering, glowing, constantly changing colors of the aurora are among the most beautiful sights of color in the sky.

The Scriptures assure us that God's spiritual realm is just as colorful as the physical universe. When John, the seer of the Apocalypse, saw heaven opened, he saw a throne set in heaven, and the One who sat upon the throne glittered like a jasper stone (a diamond), "and there was a rainbow round about the throne, in sight like unto an emerald" (Rev. 4:3). For the believer in Christ the world to come will be an experience of remarkable color, for John describes the future heavenly city, whose light was like a precious stone, "even like a jasper stone, clear as crystal" (Rev. 21:11). John describes the foundations of the city as adorned with a sparkling array of precious stones—sapphire, emerald, topaz, amethyst, among others. Consider how magnificently colorful the future home of believers is to be. The prophet Isaiah portrayed the same scene of splendor when he said, "The sun shall be no more thy light by day; neither for brightness shall the moon give light unto thee: but the Lord shall be unto thee an everlasting light, and thy God thy glory" (Isa. 60:19).

For every house is builded by some man;
but he that built all things is God

HEBREWS 3:4

Galaxy in Coma Berenices NGC 4565

THE DESIGN OF
THE UNIVERSE

The entire universe is an example of design. It manifests structure and order that only the intelligent purpose of a personal Creator can account for. A famous astronomer once said, "The picture of the world, as drawn in existing physical theories, shows arrangement of the individual elements for which the odds are a google [one with one hundred zeros after it] to one against an origin by chance." He added that if someone could sweep all idea of personal design out of the universe, he could sweep it only so far. If he traveled far enough back in time, he would find the sweepings of design "all piled up like a high wall and forming a boundary—a beginning of time."[1] There is no adequate explanation for the design and structure of the universe other than the one Scripture gives: "In the beginning God created the heaven and the earth" (Gen. 1:1).

Since we take Creation as an article of faith, it is interesting that there are striking similarities in the structure of the universe that recur again and again from the smallest parts of the universe to the largest. It is only natural that God should have a basic design, the pattern of which keeps recurring.

Let us begin with the smallest parts of the universe. It is hard to conceive that something like the head of a pin has billions upon billions of atoms in it and that although it feels solid it is mostly empty space. Everything that we can see or feel is made up of innumerable atoms. Scientists have discovered that the atom is made up of a central nucleus in which most of the mass is concentrated and around which electrons are revolving. For the most part the atom is simply empty space. If the nucleus of

[1] A. S. Eddington, *Nature*, 127, 447-453.

an atom could be enlarged to the size of a marble, the corresponding dimensions of the atom would show the electrons to be the size of tennis balls, but they would be revolving around the nucleus from a distance of a half mile away!

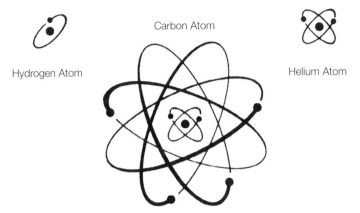

Hydrogen Atom

Carbon Atom

Helium Atom

Atoms

The structure of the atom is that of a miniature solar system. There are differences, of course, because of the differing nature and purpose of the processes involved. The solar system is a physical or mechanical system, whereas the atom is an electrical system with vast energy and speed. For example, scientists estimate that an electron circles its nucleus six quadrillion times every second. In comparison the planets revolve around the sun at a very leisurely pace. Then too, electrons revolve around the nucleus in many different planes, giving the atom a spherical shape, whereas the planets revolve around the sun in one plane, giving the solar system a comparatively flat shape. In the atom the nucleus and the electrons are much the same size, but the sun is much larger than the planets. Nevertheless, both systems have a central nucleus and, at great distance from it, a group of planets or electrons that revolves around the nucleus in a series of definite orbits. Like the solar system, the atom is mostly empty space.

It was a great day for science when this pattern was perceived in the solar system. It is well known that the astronomer

Copernicus was the first to demonstrate that the sun is the nucleus of our solar system around which the planets revolve at their respective distances. It is not so generally recognized that the planets themselves are miniature "solar systems" with moons revolving around them even as they revolve around the sun.

The largest example of the pattern is the galaxy. All the stars we can see in the night sky are grouped together in space into a flat pancake-like shape we call the Milky Way Galaxy. When we look at the Milky Way, we are looking out through the edge of our galaxy past so many stars that the sky is hazy with their light. When we look at other areas of the sky, we are looking out through the flat side of our galaxy.

Another galaxy in the constellation Coma Berenices, seen edge-on, will give a good idea of the shape of a galaxy. There are billions of stars in this galaxy just as there are in our own. If our sun were a star in this galaxy, when we would look out through the edge of the galaxy we would see a similar Milky Way; in the other directions we would see the darker parts of the sky. The stars are grouped thickly in a central nucleus and thin out as they reach the edges. Here again we can recognize the pattern which we have found in the atom and the solar system. The galaxy is the largest element of the universe that we can analyze, and here, too, we see the central nucleus, but with billions of stars circling around it instead of just a few planets.

Everything that science has examined is in motion. All the particles that make up atoms are spinning as well as revolving around the nucleus. The planets are rotating as well as revolving around the sun. The stars are rotating as well as moving in their galaxies around the central nucleus, and galaxies themselves are moving through space. Motion seems to be the rule in the universe. Nothing is standing still.

It is a little easier to perceive the motion of the stars when we see a galaxy flat side on. The famous Whirlpool Galaxy astronomers have catalogued as M 51. It happens to have a smaller satellite galaxy connected with it. In a galaxy like this it is easy to see the dense central nucleus made up of billions of stars that gradually thin out toward the edges in great spiral arms. This is one of the most beautiful and symmetrical sights in the universe. Our own Milky Way Galaxy would look similar to this, if we could just get far enough out of it to look down on it. If this were our galaxy, our sun would be located toward the edge in one of the spiral arms, which is one reason the Milky Way looks brighter in some parts of the sky than it does in others. We have to look past more stars in some directions than we do in others.

A galaxy such as ours is so huge in size that it taxes our imagination to visualize it. Astronomers estimate that there are a hundred billion stars in our galaxy spread out over such an immense distance that it would take light, traveling at the rate of more than 186,000 miles a second, 100,000 years to pass from one side of our galaxy to the other. Our sun is estimated to be about 27,000 light-years from the center of the galaxy. Even though the sun is traveling in its orbit around the galaxy at a rate of 140 miles a second, it would take our sun more than 200 million years to revolve around the nucleus and to come back to where it is now. This time measurement, currently estimated to be 225 million years, is often called the galactic year.

All the stars which we can see in the night sky belong to our own Milky Way Galaxy. The early astronomers were long puzzled by the blurred patches of light which they discovered with their elementary telescopes, but the modern telescopes show these to be other galaxies in vast numbers and at great distances from us. In fact, modern deep sky photographs show great clusters of galaxies. The unaided eye could not see a single object in the area of such a photograph. But as the photographic plate is exposed hour after hour by a telescope kept trained on this part of the sky, this host of island universes slowly takes shape.

Although there is such an immense number of galaxies, they almost always show a rather well-defined central nucleus of stars

Galaxies in Corona Borealis

around which great numbers of stars are revolving, gradually thinning out toward the edges of the galaxy. Astronomers have now photographed so many galaxies that they are able to classify them according to some commonly recurring types. Some galaxies have small spiral arms and a larger nucleus; others, a larger and better developed spiral structure; and still others, a vast and beautiful pinwheel effect in their spiral arms. The barred spiral galaxies are a corresponding variation of each type. Other galaxies have an elliptical structure.

Types of Galaxies

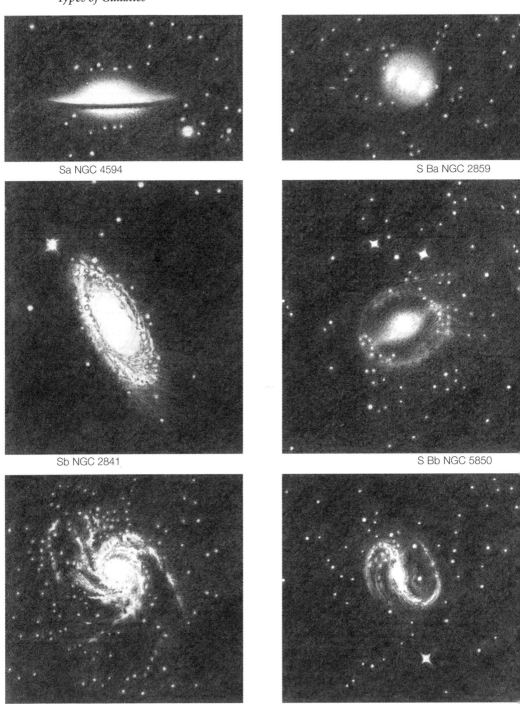

Sa NGC 4594

S Ba NGC 2859

Sb NGC 2841

S Bb NGC 5850

Sc NGC 5457 (M 101)

S Bc NGC 7479

God has not created these galaxies in a haphazard manner. A great spiral galaxy such as M 101 cannot be the handiwork of a cold, impersonal force. Whether we view the largest or the smallest part of God's creation, we can observe His workmanship, His care, and His providence in it all. It took a great Designer to construct something of such a size as this galaxy, which would yet have such beauty. No one would think of attributing the workmanship of a fine watch or other timepiece to chance. Neither will chance explain the existence of such beautiful precision as this.

Consider how intricate the structure of the universe is. The atom is made up of a central nucleus of protons and neutrons with a system of electrons circling around it. Now it is possible that the subatomic particles such as positrons and mesons and many others are circling still smaller systems in which they are involved, but here we are at the outskirts of scientific investigation, and, hence, we must await further discoveries. However, it

Galaxy M 101

is unquestioned that everything that we know in the physical universe is made up of these atomic particles that revolve as the solar system does.

Our own planet, Earth, is a central nucleus with the moon revolving around it. Most of the planets such as Mars, Jupiter, Saturn, and others have moons that revolve around them. But all the planets themselves are revolving around the sun, which is the central nucleus of the solar system. The sun, along with billions of other stars, is revolving around the central nucleus of our Milky Way Galaxy. The amazing complexity of so many systems within systems, each one complete in itself but still comprising part of a larger system, is astounding evidence for the pattern that the great Designer of the universe has employed to give unity to His creation. "For every house is builded by some man; but he that built all things is God" (Heb. 3:4).

The purpose of God, however, goes far beyond the design of the physical universe. It includes the existence of all the personalities which inhabit His universe. Consider the distance of the earth from the sun (about 93 million miles). If the earth were much closer to the sun, the heat it would absorb would make life as we know it impossible. If, on the other hand, the earth were much farther away from the sun, it would be too cold to support the kind of life which is found on the earth. Clearly, the relationship between the sun and the earth is the most beneficial possible for life and particularly for man. Not only is our God great enough to create the universe, but He is also great enough to know about and to be concerned with the smallest part of His creation. The Bible tells us that not even the obscure sparrow can escape the notice of God; how much more does God care for man, who is created in His own image?

God's purpose was formulated before He began His creation, and He will see it consummated to the fullest extent. It is this God, says the Apostle Paul, "who hath saved us, and called us with an holy calling, not according to our works, but according to his own purpose and grace, which was given us in Christ Jesus before the world began, but is now made manifest by the appearing of our Saviour Jesus Christ, who hath abolished death, and hath brought life and immortality to light through the gospel" (II Tim. 1:9-10).

AND THE ELEMENTS SHALL MELT WITH FERVENT HEAT

II PETER 3:10

THE END OF
THE WORLD

Everyone at some time has pondered the question of how this world will come to an end. "The end of the world" is a popular science fiction theme. However, very sober astronomy textbooks have chapters with such titles as "The Life and Death of the Sun," "The Birth and Demise of Stars," "The Origin and End of the Galaxy," or "The Evolution of the Universe." Most of these studies are highly speculative and strongly evolutionary. The Scripture also has much to say about the origin and end of the world.

It is not possible to discuss the end of the world without paying some attention to its beginning. So we will consider the whole of cosmology: the study of the origin and end of the universe. Some people think that science has a great advantage in considering such questions, but in reality science is at a great disadvantage here. In fact, whether cosmology can be called a science at all is an open question. Science is usually defined as the study of processes or facts that can be observed, empirically tested, and proved. But by the nature of the case no men were observers of the origin of the world, and none can observe its end. It is not possible to run a test of either how the world originated or how it will end. These are unique events.

A person who is an evolutionist must believe that the world originated spontaneously and will come to an end without the help or concern of an Almighty God. The creationist, on the other hand, believes that God created the world and will bring it to an appropriate consummation. Either belief is a matter of faith. Indeed, it takes much more faith to believe in evolution than it takes to believe in Creation by an omnipotent God. The

Christian holds that Creation is the most reasonable explanation for the purposive design, order, and beauty of the universe. There is no adequate explanation for the design and structure of the universe other than that given by Scripture: "In the beginning God created the heaven and the earth" (Gen. 1:1).

Let us explore the vastness of the universe for evidence of how the world began and how it will end. First, we raise the question of where all the stars came from. Evolutionists advance several theories. One of these is the so-called "steady state" theory, which holds that matter spontaneously originates throughout space. In effect this view deifies the universe, making it an infinite, self-sustaining entity. However, the evidence is piling up against this view so seriously that even its advocates now admit that it is probably wrong. A more popular view is the so-called "big bang" theory. However, this view makes no attempt to explain the origin of anything; it assumes the existence of all the matter in the universe at the very "beginning." It merely attempts to explain how the matter reached its present form. Its advocates claim that the "primeval atom," or "cosmic egg," blew up and in doing so blew out of itself all the stars and galaxies we now see. Evolutionists sometimes admit "as regards the origin of the 'primaeval fireball,' the biblical theory still remains almost as good as any other that can be conjured up by human imagination."[1] It takes great faith to believe that a random explosion created all the order and symmetry of the universe. It is especially difficult since all matter is supposed to start out as neutrons, which form hydrogen atoms that rapidly "build up" into the heavier elements in the first 30 minutes of the explosion. One of the big problems with this view is that although neutrons can build up into a helium-four nucleus rapidly, it is almost impossible for them to go beyond this stage. And other neutrons attaching themselves to the helium-four nucleus would break down again

---

[1] Zdenek Kopal, *Man and His Universe* (New York: William Morrow, 1972), 292.

in less than a billionth of a second. Even advocates of the theory admit that this gap seems insuperable.[2]

Evolutionists also think that stars were formed by conglomerations of dust and gas like the diffuse nebulae seen throughout the universe. According to their theory, the dust and gas condensed together and contracted until the temperature and pressure were right to start a hydrogen reaction that would light the star. However, gas tends to disperse rather than condense, especially in the near vacuum of outer space and especially in view of the tremendous explosion that is supposed to have started its outward motion.

Observing stars in large galactic groups, some evolutionists think that galaxies evolve into different forms. The astronomer Hubble classified galaxies into spiral galaxies, barred spirals, and elliptical galaxies, with subclasses of each. His classification was simply a description of the kinds of galaxies astronomers had observed. Hubble thought that galaxies evolve from the elliptical types into the spiral types. Most modern evolutionists think rather that the spiral galaxies evolve into the elliptical types. Today more sober scientists state bluntly, "We remain without any real indication that galaxies evolve at all."[3] Our present information indicates that galaxies were formed at the same time. A better explanation is that God created all the varieties of galaxies, and that their present structure manifests the handiwork of a personal God rather than the effects of a random explosion.

What will be the end of these far-flung hosts of galaxies? The "steady state" theory holds that matter is continually being created and that galaxies will continue to be formed as they spread out in the universe. Most astronomers do not follow this theory.

[2] Isaac Asimov, *The Universe: From Flat Earth to Quasar* (New York: Walker, 1966), 216.

[3] Robert T. Dixon, *Dynamic Astronomy* (Englewood Cliffs, N.J.: Prentice-Hall, 1971), 300.

The "big bang" theory holds that stars will gradually exhaust their supplies of nuclear energy; their nuclear reactions will one day shut down; and the stars of the galaxies will one by one wink out. The galaxies, then composed of darkened radioactive ash balls, will continue hurtling onward through space forever. Some evolutionists think that the universe is oscillating. The galaxies that are now hurtling outward must be stopped by some unknown force and then hurtle back together again to form another "cosmic egg," which will explode in another "big bang." Thus the universe explodes and collapses forever in an 80-billion-year cycle. Aside from the inherent difficulties of an explosion forming any clear structures from the atom to the galaxies, there is no known force that could stop the outward rush of the galaxies and cause them to fall inward again.

Great Comet of 1861

About the only good word that the evolutionist can say about the future is that man will not be around to see the end. Long before the galaxy burns out, our own sun will destroy all life on the earth. The sun shines now because of a thermonuclear reaction that converts hydrogen into helium. Eventually, most of the central core of the sun will be helium; the hydrogen will be in a shell around the core. As the hydrogen reaction diminishes, the central core will contract. This contraction will raise the temperature enough to start the hydrogen reaction in the shell of the sun. Instead of the sun's growing dimmer and smaller, the shell of the sun will expand tremendously as the sun becomes a red giant. The sun may very well become larger than the orbit of Mercury or Venus around the present sun. On Earth the oceans will boil dry. All life will perish from the intense heat of the giant sun. The only comforting thought is that this disaster is about five billion years in the future![4] After the sun passes through this giant stage, it will gradually contract into a white dwarf, and after a period in this diminished condition, it will finally shut down the nuclear reaction and become a black dwarf, entirely invisible. The solar system will be dead.

This evolutionary portrait of the universe's future has left out one very important element: God. The Lord God is not going to allow this universe simply to run down and expire into a dismal ash heap. The portrait that the Scriptures give concerning the future is far more glorious and satisfactory. The Bible tells us that this present age will end with living believers being caught up in resurrection glory to meet the Lord in the air (I Thess. 4:17). Afterward on earth will be the Great Tribulation period in which God shall visit His wrath upon the unbelieving men on earth. During this tribulation period an angel will pour out his bowl of wrath on the sun and men will be "scorched with great heat" and blaspheme God, who "hath power over these plagues"; they will not repent to give Him glory (Rev. 16:9). The sun may well be used as an instrument of divine wrath, but it will not be used to end life on earth. God will bring the tribulation period to a close and will introduce the Millennium, in which the Lord Jesus Christ will reign over the earth in perfect peace and righteousness. After the millennial

---

[4] John Rublowsky, *Life and Death of the Sun* (New York: Basic Books, 1964), 113-14.

reign, men will be judged before the Great White Throne according to their relationship with the Lord Jesus Christ. The elements shall melt—that is, be loosed—with fervent heat. There will be an atomic reorganization of all the universe (II Pet. 3:10). God will fashion a new heaven and a new earth (Rev. 21:1). All impurities will be removed; sin will be a thing of the past; the redeemed company will live in the presence of the Lord Jesus Christ in the holy city. "And the city had no need of the sun, neither of the moon, to shine in it: for the glory of God did lighten it, and the Lamb is the light thereof" (Rev. 21:23). The glory of God will illumine all creation. The entire universe will be brought to its perfect consummation to the glory of God.

Now, may I address the reader with a personal word? If you are not sure that you know the Creator of the universe, the Lord Jesus Christ, as your personal Savior, I invite you to put your faith in Him right now. The Lord Jesus Himself invites you, "Come unto me, all ye that labour and are heavy laden, and I will give you rest. Take my yoke upon you, and learn of me; for I am meek and lowly in heart: and ye shall find rest unto your souls" (Matt. 11:28-29). The Scriptures clearly promise, "Believe on the Lord Jesus Christ, and thou shalt be saved" (Acts 16:31). Only the Lord Jesus Christ can forgive sin, provide salvation, and give assurance of eternal life in the glories of the world to come. "Neither is there salvation in any other: for there is none other name under heaven given among men, whereby we must be saved" (Acts 4:12). A glorious future awaits those who look forward to a new heaven and a new earth with a redeemed company of just men made perfect.

LET NOW THE ASTROLOGERS, THE STARGAZERS, THE
MONTHLY PROGNOSTICATORS, STAND UP, AND SAVE
THEE FROM THESE THINGS THAT SHALL COME UPON
THEE

ISAIAH 47:13

THE ERROR OF ASTROLOGY

Astronomers are horrified when someone refers to their field as "astrology." Astronomy is a science, but astrology is a superstition. Not only do men of science deprecate astrology, but the Bible also has some very harsh words to say against it. God challenges the astrologers of ancient Babylon to deliver their nation from the judgment that God is bringing upon them: "You are wearied with your many counsels; let now the astrologers, those who prophesy by the stars, those who predict by the new moons, stand up and save you from what will come upon you. Behold, they have become like stubble, fire burns them; they cannot deliver themselves from the power of the flame" (Isa. 47:13-14 NASV). The astrologers of ancient Babylon had no power to foresee the judgments that God was going to inflict upon their nation or to deliver themselves from the disasters when they came. If the claims of astrology were true, its adherents would live in a secure knowledge of the future, but it is evident that the adherents of astrology are afflicted by the slings of fortune in the same way that all mankind is.

The prophet Daniel reminded King Nebuchadnezzar that "the wise men, the astrologers, the magicians, the soothsayers" could not show the king what his dream meant, "but there is a God in heaven that revealeth secrets, and maketh known to the king Nebuchadnezzar what shall be in the latter days" (Dan. 2:27-28). The astrologers were utterly powerless to answer the king's questions, but Daniel was a prophet of the true God, who does indeed reveal the future to His servants in His Word. Today, God's Word is still the proper place to seek guidance and insight for the circumstances of life.

How do astrologers make their followers think they have supernatural insight and powers? Astrologers maintain that the positions of the sun, moon, and planets in relation to the stars at the moment of a person's birth determine his destiny. They divide the paths of these heavenly bodies by the twelve regions of the zodiac, which they identify by the constellations that appear in these regions. For example, if a person is born between March 21 and April 19, astrologers say that he is an "Aries" because the sun is then in the constellation Aries in relation to the earth. Actually, the sun is not in the constellation Aries at that time. Because of the motion of the earth, called the precession of the equinoxes, the sun is really in the constellation Pisces. Over 2,000 years ago the sun was in Aries during these days, but since then it has been in Pisces. Astrologers try to explain away this problem by saying that they are calculating on the basis of the sign of Aries rather than the constellation. This easy answer, however, does not solve the problem, because to the ancient astrologers the signs and the constellations were the same thing. The calculations of the ancient and the modern astrologers thus cannot both be right. In adhering to the ancient zodiacal calendar, modern astrologers are calculating on the basis of an erroneous conception of the position of the heavenly bodies.

Furthermore, if it be true that the position of the sun, moon, and planets absolutely determines a person's destiny, why do persons born at the same moment not have the same destiny? Even identical twins born within seconds of one another may have very different characters and destinies.

When casting a person's horoscope, professional astrologers often use such general statements that they cannot help being right on some matters. There are over 2,000 newspapers and magazines in the United States that regularly carry columns on astrology. These horoscopes contain such advice as "today you must be careful in your business dealings." Everyone can profit from such advice, because there is no day in which one can afford to be careless about his business. They make such predictions as "you will need patience today." Obviously, there is never a day in which one does not need patience. The followers of these columns seize upon such advice; watch for the first possible need for it; and, when it comes (as it surely will), feel that astrology is completely vindicated in the events that follow. This inference is a logical fallacy called *post hoc* reasoning (*post hoc, ergo propter hoc,* "after this, therefore because of this"). The astrologer reasons on the same level as a person who, having seen a black cat cross his path, attributes the next occurrence of "bad luck" to the appearance of the black cat. Both inferences are simply superstition.

The truth of the matter is that God has created the sun, moon, planets, and stars and has caused them to move through space in the accomplishment of His purpose. The heavenly bodies are no more a cause of earthly events than are black cats. The real question to ask is, "Who is lord of one's life?" If a person comes to a saving faith in the Lord Jesus Christ, his destiny is not immutably set by the position of heavenly bodies. The Lord of the universe is providentially ordering all things for the benefit of His child. For "we know that all things work together for good to them that love God, to them who are the called according to his purpose" (Rom. 8:28).

Some astrologers cite the verse "the stars in their courses fought against Sisera" (Judg. 5:20). What does this passage mean? Judges 5 is a poem, a song of praise, for the Lord's deliverance of the Israelites through Deborah and Barak. What this passage really means is that the Lord God defeated the enemies of Israel. In the Lord's providential control, not only the armies of Israel but even nature was opposing the kings of Canaan. The river Kishon overflowed and swept away the chariots of Sisera (Judg. 5:21). The Bible is in no way teaching that an impersonal destiny was opposed to Sisera's forces but rather that the personal God of heaven and earth was judging the enemies of Israel.

A person who recognizes that he needs guidance for his daily affairs should turn to the Word of God. King David urged confidence in the leading of God. "Let all those that seek thee rejoice and be glad in thee: and let such as love thy salvation say continually, Let God be magnified" (Ps. 70:4). The Word of God provides more effective guidance than any guesses of astrologers. The Apostle Peter tells us, "We have also a more sure word of prophecy; whereunto ye do well that ye take heed, as unto a light that shineth in a dark place, until the day dawn, and the day star arise in your hearts" (II Pet. 1:19). The Lord Jesus commanded, "Search the scriptures" (John 5:39). The book of Acts calls the Bereans "more noble" because they searched the Scriptures daily (Acts 17:11). God has provided His Word to give His people the spiritual insight and guidance that they need. He invites them to seek Himself for guidance and counsel: "If any of you lack wisdom, let him ask of God, that giveth to all men liberally, and upbraideth not; and it shall be given him" (James 1:5). The psalmist's words remain true that "Thy word is a lamp unto my feet, and a light unto my path" (Ps. 119:105). His vast creation is a testimony to the wisdom and power of God. "The heavens declare the glory of God; and the firmament sheweth his handywork" (Ps. 19:1).

STUDY HELPS

	Mass (10^{21} tons)	Diameter (miles)	Density (lbs/ft³)	Gravity (ft/s³)	Escape Velocity (miles/s)	Rotation Period (hours)	Length of Day (hours)	Distance from Sun (10^6 miles)	Perihelion (10^6 miles)
Mercury	0.364	3032	339	12.1	2.7	1407.6	4222.6	36.0	28.6
Venus	5.37	7521	327	29.1	6.4	-5832.5	2802.0	67.2	66.8
Earth	6.58	7926	344	32.1	7.0	23.9	24.0	93.0	91.4
Moon	0.081	2159	209	5.3	1.5	655.7	708.7	0.239*	0.226*
Mars	0.708	4222	246	12.1	3.1	24.6	24.7	141.6	128.4
Jupiter	2093	88,846	83	75.9	37.0	9.9	9.9	483.8	460.1
Saturn	627	74,897	43	29.4	22.1	10.7	10.7	890.8	840.4
Uranus	95.7	31,763	79	28.5	13.2	-17.2	17.2	1784.8	1703.4
Neptune	113	30,775	102	36.0	14.6	16.1	16.1	2793.1	2761.6
Pluto	0.0138	1485	110	1.9	0.7	-153.3	153.3	3647.2	2755.8

*relative to Earth

PLANETARY FACT SHEET
U.S. UNITS

Aphelion (10⁶ miles)	Orbital Period (days)	Orbital Velocity (miles/s)	Orbital Inclination (degrees)	Orbital Eccentricity	Axial Tilt (degrees)	Mean Temperature (F)	Surface Pressure (atmospheres)	Number of Moons	Ring System	Global Magnetic Field
43.4	88.0	29.7	7.0	0.205	0.01	333	0	0	No	Yes
67.7	224.7	21.8	3.4	0.007	177.4	867	91	0	No	No
94.5	365.2	18.5	0.0	0.017	23.5	59	1	1	No	Yes
0.252	27.3	0.64	5.1	0.055	6.7	-4	0	0	No	No
154.9	687.0	15.0	1.9	0.094	25.2	-85	0.01	2	No	No
507.4	4331	8.1	1.3	0.049	3.1	-166	**	38	Yes	Yes
941.1	10,747	6.0	2.5	0.057	26.7	-220	**	39	Yes	Yes
1866.4	30,589	4.2	0.8	0.046	97.8	-320	**	20	Yes	Yes
2824.5	59,800	3.4	1.8	0.011	28.3	-330	**	8	Yes	Yes
4538.7	90,588	2.9	17.2	0.244	122.5	-375	0	1	No	**

**Unknown

199

CONCORDANCE OF ASTRONOMY IN THE BIBLE

Bear (Arcturus) (2)
Job 9:9; 38:32
Host (16)
Deuteronomy 4:19; 17:3; II
Kings 17:16; 21:3; 21:5; 23:4;
23:5; II Chronicles 33:3; 33:5;
Isaiah 34:4; Jeremiah 8:2; 19:13;
33:22; Daniel 8:10; Zephaniah
1:5; Acts 7:42
Lights (5)
Genesis 1:14; 1:15; 1:16 (3)
Mazzaroth (1)
Job 38:32
Moon (61)
Genesis 37:9; Deuteronomy
4:19; 17:3; 33:14; Joshua 10:12;
10:13; I Samuel 20:5; 20:18;
20:24; II Kings 4:23; 23:5; I
Chronicles 23:31; II Chronicles
2:4; 8:13; 31:3; Ezra 3:5;
Nehemiah 10:33; Job 25:5;
31:26; Psalms 8:3; 72:5; 72:7;
81:3; 89:37; 104:19; 121:6; 136:9;
148:3; Ecclesiastes 12:2; Song of
Solomon 6:10; Isaiah 1:13; 1:14;
13:10; 24:23; 30:26; 60:19; 60:20;
66:23; Jeremiah 8:2; 31:35;
Ezekiel 32:7; 45:17; 46:1; 46:3;
46:6; Hosea 2:11; Joel 2:10; 2:31;
3:15; Amos 8:5; Habakkuk 3:11;
Matthew 24:29; Mark 13:24;
Luke 21:25; Acts 2:20; I
Corinthians 15:41; Colossians
2:16; Revelation 6:12; 8:12; 12:1;
21:23

Orion (3)
Job 9:9; 38:31; Amos 5:8
Planets (1)
II Kings 23:5
Pleiades (2)
Job 9:9; 38:31
Star (66)
Genesis 1:16; 15:5; 22:17; 26:4;
37:9; Exodus 32:13; Numbers
24:17; Deuteronomy 1:10; 4:19;
10:22; 28:62; Judges 5:20; I
Chronicles 27:23; Nehemiah
4:21; 9:23; Job 3:9; 9:7; 22:12;
25:5; 38:7; Psalms 8:3; 136:9;
147:4; 148:3; Ecclesiastes 12:2;
Isaiah 13:10; 14:13; 47:13;
Jeremiah 31:35; Ezekiel 32:7;
Daniel 8:10; 12:3; Joel 2:10; 3:15;
Amos 5:8; 5:26; Obadiah 4;
Nahum 3:16; Matthew 2:2; 2:7;
2:9; 2:10; 24:29; Mark 13:25;
Luke 21:25; Acts 7:43; 27:20; I
Corinthians 15:41 (2); Hebrews
11:12; II Peter 1:19; Jude 13;
Revelation 1:16; 1:20 (2); 2:1;
2:28; 3:1; 6:13; 8:10; 8:11; 8:12;
9:1; 12:1; 12:4; 22:16
Sun (158)
Genesis 15:12; 15:17; 19:23;
28:11; 32:31; 37:9; Exodus 16:21;
17:12; 22:3; 22:26; Leviticus
22:7; Numbers 25:4;
Deuteronomy 4:19; 11:30; 16:6;
17:3; 23:11; 24:13; 24:15; 33:14;
Joshua 1:4; 8:29; 10:12; 10:13

(2); 10:27; 12:1; Judges 5:31; 8:13; 9:33; 14:18; 19:14; I Samuel 11:9; II Samuel 2:24; 3:35; 12:11; 12:12; 23:4; I Kings 22:36; II Kings 3:22; 23:5; 23:11 (2); II Chronicles 18:34; Nehemiah 7:3; Job 8:16; 9:7; 30:28; 31:26; Psalms 19:4; 50:1; 58:8; 72:5; 72:17; 74:16; 84:11; 89:36; 104:19; 104:22; 113:3; 121:6; 136:8; 148:3; Ecclesiastes 1:3; 1:5 (2); 1:9; 1:14; 2:11; 2:17; 2:18; 2:19; 2:20; 2:22; 3:16; 4:1; 4:3; 4:7; 4:15; 5:13; 5:18; 6:1; 6:5; 6:12; 7:11; 8:9; 8:15 (2); 8:17; 9:3; 9:6; 9:9 (2); 9:11; 9:13; 10:5; 11:7; 12:2; Song of Solomon 1:6; 6:10; Isaiah 13:10; 24:23; 30:26; 38:8 (2); 41:25; 45:6; 49:10; 59:19; 60:19; 60:20; Jeremiah 8:2; 15:9; 31:35; Ezekiel 8:16; 32:7; Daniel 6:14; Joel 2:10; 2:31; 3:15; Amos 8:9; Jonah 4:8 (2); Habakkuk 3:11; Micah 3:6; Nahum 3:17; Malachi 1:11; 4:2; Matthew 5:45; 13:6; 13:43; 17:2; 24:29; Mark 1:32; 4:6; 13:24; 16:2; Luke 4:40; 21:25; 23:45; Acts 2:20; 13:11; 26:13; 27:20; I Corinthians 15:41; Ephesians 4:26; James 1:11; Revelation 1:16; 6:12; 7:16; 8:12; 9:2; 10:1; 12:1; 16:8; 19:17; 21:23; 22:5

BIBLIOGRAPHY

I. Devotional works on the stars and Scripture

Brackbill, Maurice Thaddeus. *The Heavens Declare.* Chicago: Moody, 1959.
128 pp.
> Brief devotional meditations. He discusses the sun, the stars,
> exploding stars; believes that the stars are billions of years old
> (pp. 65ff.); urges seeing God in nature (pp. 101ff.).

Lyon, Thoburn C. *Witness in the Sky.* Chicago: Moody, 1961. 128 pp.
> Brief devotional studies in the beauty of the stars, their distance,
> countless number, power, etc. He holds to theistic evolution (pp.
> 75-81); argues that the material universe witnesses to the exis-
> tence of God (pp. 114ff.).

Maunder, E. Walter. *The Astronomy of the Bible.* London: Hodder and
Stoughton, 1909. 410 pp.
> Professional comments on the references to astronomy in the
> Bible. He covers creation, the deep, the firmament, the sun, the
> moon, stars, comets, constellations, Leviathan, Orion, the
> Pleiades, Mazzaroth, time, the cycles of Daniel, Joshua's long day,
> the dial of Ahaz, the star of Bethlehem.

Unger, Merrill F. *Starlit Paths for Pilgrim Feet.* Findlay, Ohio: Dunham, 1958.
192 pp.
> Devotional studies in select biblical references to the stars. He
> covers angels as morning stars; the darkness of sin and Satan;
> evening stars; storms and stars; the bright, the morning star; star-
> like saints.

II. Works useful for identifying stars and constellations

Baker, Robert. *Introducing the Constellations.* New York: Viking, 1957.

Chartrand, Mark R. *National Audubon Society Field Guide to the Night Sky.*
New York: Alfred A. Knopf, 1991, 2001.

Chartrand, Mark R. *Night Sky: A Field Guide to the Heavens.* Golden Field
Guides. New York: St. Martin's Press, 1990.

Menzel, Donald. *A Field Guide to the Stars and Planets.* Boston: Houghton
Mifflin, 1964.

Norton, Arthur. *A Star Atlas.* Cambridge: Sky Publishing, 1978.
   The most thorough and complete star charts.

Ridpath, Ian. *Stars and Planets.* Princeton, N.J.: Princeton University Press, 1984, 2001.

Rükl, Antonin. *Constellation Guidebook.* New York: Sterling Publishing, Inc., 1996.

Sidgwick, J. B. *Amateur Astronomer's Handbook.* New York: Dover Publications, 1980.

Astronomy. A periodical with monthly star charts. Waukesha, WI: Kalmbach Publishing. http://www.astronomy.com

Sky and Telescope. A periodical with monthly star charts. Cambridge, MA: Sky Publishing Corporation. http://www.SkyandTelescope.com

Sky News. The Canadian Magazine of Astronomy & Stargazing with bimonthly star charts. http://www.skynewsmagazine.com

III. Standard works for amateur astronomy (often with strong bias toward evolutionary theories)

Cole, Franklyn W. *Fundamental Astronomy.* New York: Wiley, 1974. 476 pp.

Eicher, David J. *Deep-Sky Observing With Small Telescopes.* Hillside, N.J.: Enslow Publishers, Inc., 1989. 336 pp.

Paul, Henry E. *Outer Space Photography for the Amateur.* New York: Amphoto, 1960. 124 pp.

Ridpath, Ian. *An Introduction to Astronomy.* New York: Todtry Productions, 1999. 80 pp.

Sherrod, P. Clay. *A Complete Manual of Amateur Astronomy.* Englewood Cliffs, N.J.: Prentice-Hall, 1981. 319 pp.

Wyatt, Stanley. *Principles of Astronomy.* Boston: Allyn and Bacon, 1971. 686 pp.

IV. Historical studies in astronomy

Allen, Richard Hinckley. *Star Names: Their Lore and Meaning.* 1899; rpt. New York: Dover, 1963. 563 pp.

Boorstin, Daniel J. *The Discoverers.* New York: Random House, 1983. 745 pp.

Hawkins, Gerald. *Splendor in the Sky.* New York: Harper, 1961.

Lockyer, J. Norman. *The Dawn of Astronomy.* 1894: rpt. Cambridge, Mass.: MIT Press, 1964. 432 pp.

Rousseau, Pierre. *Man's Conquest of the Stars.* New York: Norton, 1961.

Thiel, Rudolf. *And There Was Light.* New York: Knopf, 1957.

INDEX TO THE CONSTELLATIONS

The forty-eight ancient constellations:

Andromeda, 9, 16, 30, 40, 43, 54, 152
Aquarius, 30, 40, 49, 68
Aquila, 30, 34, 36, 40, 44, 166
Ara, 68, 72
Argo, 72
Aries, 22, 40, 50, 54
Auriga, 16, 40, 54, 56, 64, 166
Boötes, 16, 25, 30, 32, 36, 155, 166, 167
Cancer, 16, 27, 54
Canis Major, 16, 54, 61, 63, 68
Canis Minor, 16, 54, 56
Capricornus, 30, 40, 49, 68
Cassiopeia, 16, 30, 40, 45, 54
Centaurus, 8, 16, 30, 68, 71
Cepheus, 16, 30, 40, 45, 54
Cetus, 40, 54, 68, 72
Corona Australis, 68, 72
Corona Borealis, 16, 27, 30, 35, 40
Corvus, 16, 30, 68, 70
Crater,16, 68, 70
Cygnus, 9, 30, 35, 40, 42, 54, 155, 159, 166
Delphinus, 30, 40, 44
Draco, 16, 24, 27, 30, 33, 40, 45, 54
Equuleus, 40, 44
Eridanus, 54, 64, 68

Gemini, 16, 24, 25, 54, 56, 63, 166
Hercules, 16, 27, 30, 35, 40, 42
Hydra, 16, 26, 30, 54, 68
Leo, 16, 21, 25, 26, 28, 30, 32, 36, 54
Lepus, 54, 63, 64, 68
Libra, 16, 30, 36, 68
Lupus, 30, 36, 68
Lyra, 16, 30, 34, 40, 42, 156, 166
Ophiuchus, 30, 36, 40, 68
Orion, 16, 36, 54, 55, 58, 60, 63, 68, 155, 166
Pegasus, 30, 40, 43, 44, 50, 54
Perseus, 16, 40, 46, 47, 54, 64
Pisces, 22, 50, 54, 97
Piscis Austrinus, 40, 49, 50, 68
Sagitta, 30, 40, 44
Sagittarius, 30, 34, 40, 68, 155, 159
Scorpius, 28, 30, 34, 35, 68, 166
Serpens, 16, 27, 30, 36, 40, 68
Taurus, 16, 22, 24, 25, 28, 40, 54, 55, 56, 59, 60, 157, 166
Triangulum, 9, 11, 40, 44, 54, 152
Ursa Major, 16, 23, 24, 25, 30, 31, 33, 40, 54
Ursa Minor, 16, 23, 24, 30, 40, 54
Virgo, 16, 25, 28, 30, 32, 36, 68, 166

205

The forty modern constellations:

INDEX TO SCRIPTURE REFERENCES

TOPICAL INDEX

210